T0062465

Man and God

The Truth and Reality about Religion and Political Strategy of Western Power in the Middle East

Ahmad Nosrati

Order this book online at www.trafford.com
or email orders@trafford.com

Most Trafford titles are also available at major online book retailers.

Printed in Victoria, BC, Canada.

ISBN: 978-1-4269-2315-9 (Soft)
ISBN: 978-1-4269-2323-4 (Hard)

Library of Congress Control Number: 2009913219

*We at Trafford believe that it is the responsibility of us all, as both individuals
and corporations, to make choices that are environmentally and socially sound.
You, in turn, are supporting this responsible conduct each time you purchase a
Trafford book, or make use of our publishing services. To find out how you are
helping, please visit www.trafford.com/responsiblepublishing.html*

*Our mission is to efficiently provide the world's finest, most comprehensive
book publishing service, enabling every author to experience success.
To find out how to publish your book, your way, and have it available
worldwide, visit us online at www.trafford.com*

Trafford rev. 01/13/2010

 www.trafford.com

North America & international
toll-free: 1 888 232 4444 (USA & Canada)
phone: 250 383 6864 ♦ fax: 812 355 4082 ♦ email: info@trafford.com

Dedication

Parents are symbolic of true love and compassion. My father's dying words were, "My greatest concern is for Ahmad's education." My mother attempted to respond reassuringly, "Do not worry. I will try to do my best!" She then spent the next three years of her life in Najaf, Iraq, sacrificing all of her personal needs to care for me until I was finally admitted to the school of religion there and was in a position on my own to pursue my education and to be self-sufficient. I, therefore, dedicate this book in their honor: to my mother, Fatemah-Jalali, and to my father, Haji Sheik Golame Hossein Nosrati. Their names and loving devotion remain always in the depths of my heart.

Ahmad Nosrati   November 2007

Contents

Statement of Purpose

My objective in writing what has been recorded thus far has been to discover the root cause of the current conflict between Western and Middle Eastern factions, a confrontation that has been labeled a struggle for freedom against terrorism. Such a discovery may enable us to identify a solution, hopefully permanent, for the seemingly futile battle we are facing.

In making this attempt, questions have been raised; among them, foremost, Have deceptive foreign policies of the West led to a humiliation of people of the Middle East? Or has the conviction of certain radical Islamists like al Qaeda that they must kill their adversaries driven this struggle? Indeed, is all that has transpired the result of one basic cause, or are several factors at work in extending the bitterness of the situation?

Basically, the exploration into answers for these questions has been to study the history and philosophy of contending forces from the standpoint of their religious principles as they are understood by the hoi polloi as well as the intellectuals.

A second question that we have attempted to consider: is the character of God, the creator of this universe with its countless planets—like that of a king or of a president or of a corporation CEO—who attempts to maintain dominance of his creation through the endless activities of fanatical devotees, such as Hezbollah and Feda'iyan (to sacrifice) who may be considered to be backstairs operatives?

A third consideration: if not for the gigantic oil resources of the Middle East, would we be participating in this grievous present war?

A fourth quandary: had not Palestine been a colony of the British government following the First World War, would the current nation of Israel actually exist in its present location?

A fifth question: is it possible for the West to enjoy the benefits of Middle Eastern oil without utilizing the oppressive techniques of colonization, deceitful manipulation, or war?

And finally, a sixth query: are the foreign political strategies of the Western powers really acceptable to its people—the citizens of the USA or Europe and of the rest of the world?

And may I repeat, in this writing, there is no attempt to cast disrespect or to judge anyone or any group or country. Rather, this book is written with the intention of providing unbiased information to those who choose to peruse it. All those of us who can find no justification in the pursuit of actions that result in the killing of innocent human beings—be they military or civilian, in the name of God, or for the achievement of freedom and human rights—will find it interesting to deal carefully with the considerations of this text as we seek to explain the net effect of our current dilemma. It is in keeping with the solemnity of this quest that you are invited to share this wrestling of the soul with us.

Chapter One

Human Nature vs. God

Man has countless needs whereas God has absolutely no needs. Human existence is not possible without bodily and spiritual needs. Only death ends mortal need. Inasmuch as humans are created as social beings, they cannot secure these needs on their own but discover that they depend on one another for fulfillment of this need. To facilitate such fulfillment, humankind established themselves in families then widened the circle to tribes, clans, and nations. Unlike some forms of animal life, mankind is capable of cooperation and intricate interdependancy; in order to secure specific needs, individual human beings will even forfeit their own freedom to secure survival and the greater good.

Basic bodily needs are water, food, and shelter. Fundamental spiritual needs include love freedom, and acceptance. An offshoot of spiritual requirement is intellectual need, which includes knowledge, awareness, and tranquility. Without these, bodily needs cannot be provided.

The Identity of Good, Bad, and Freedom

An anthropological dilemma arises. Each group (family, clan, or tribe) thinks that their needs take preeminence and that their system of corporate action to procure their needs (their culture or mores) is superior to all others. Prejudicial thinking favoring one's own morality or religion becomes a predominant way of thinking, and the independent philosopher (or noncommitted scientist) is unable to suggest a middle way or standard that is acceptable to everyone. It becomes impossible objectively to define "good" or "bad," and antipathy between groups arises because of subjective bias. Cultural differences pose barriers to cooperation.

For example, in some groups of Tibetan culture, a woman is allowed to have five husbands at one time; and she is allowed to divorce any or all of them at whatever time she chooses. Opposite to this is the Islamic principle that any man may have four wives simultaneously or permanently but is allowed to divorce a wife at his will. A synthesis of these two doctrines becomes impossible, and permanent division stemming from diverging customs separates these groups in this cultural aspect almost irreversibly unless some global principle of acceptance and understanding prevails.

As a further example, the famous Greek historian Herodotus cited how Darius, famous Persian emperor, summoned several Greek people into his court and asked one of them how much money he might demand in order to eat the ashes of his father's body. The Greek responded, "Even if you offered me all the wealth of the world, I could never do such a thing!" whereas when he asked an Asian Indian, "Why would you cremate your father and then consume his ashes?" the Indian replied, "To do so is our cultural belief, and please do not judge it to be a horrendous practice." The extremely antipodal responses to this query fulfilled the attempt Darius was making to teach his Persian subjects that they should expect great differences in cultures and, further, that they should have respect for the beliefs and practices of all. Even as Herodotus came to the conclusion that each group considered their beliefs and practices to be the most proper, Darius was trying to teach his courtesans to be strictly nonjudgmental and to adhere to the teaching of Zoroastrians, namely, to observe others and to see no evil, to hear no evil, and to speak no evil concerning their mores. In so doing, they would achieve the moral ideal of treating others kindly and as they themselves would expect to be treated. For Darius, this was the true meaning of "freedom of religion," a principle to which he strongly subscribed; and without such freedom, there could also be no freedom of thought nor any progress in the world.

It is well to make a brief aside here. Just as there are diverse linguistic differences acceptable to the many people on this planet, so also must we accept many moral differences. Now and then, better that we cooperate and practice respect for these variations than that we try to apply some gauge of good and evil to them and create a critical standoff. An agreeable attitude will allow further communication, and only by such interaction will our countless needs be addressed.

Biologists advise us that each human body is formed from seventy trillion cells. Each of these cells has independent genetic function. Much energy is expended to keep the individual cells in communication with the other cells. Interrelated activity among these cells keeps the entire body healthy and functioning normally. When one cell cannot cooperate with the others due to affliction with outside invaders (virus or bacteria) or inner malfunction (cancer), it must expend its energy fighting with these destructors. Either it defeats them and survives to cooperate again, or it is defeated and drops out of the race. Again, the point is that the cells function independently as well as have independent needs.

And each of these seventy trillion cells must be fed in order to remain healthy. Without food, they will not be able to survive, fight off invaders, or correct inner malfunction. Ensuing weakness because of starvation will cause sickness or death—the anthem of interdependence uttered by Saint Paul in the letter to the Corinthians. We humans on this planet are just like one of the seventy trillion cells of the body—we all require cooperation with one another to remain viable.

Ghazali, a tenth-century Iranian philosopher, also made this comment: "Do you think that you are insignificant in the universe? No, the universe is set up within you!" His emphasis again underscores the principles of interdependency and mutuality. Abraham Lincoln phrased this reasoning as "All humans are created equal." Earlier Greek philosophers approached the subject with a slightly different attitude; Aristotle (500–400 BC) allowed that some humans are created as slaves and servants while some are born as governors or rulers. His Socratic disciple Plato (of the following century), however, summarized the thought in the phrase "Might is right." For Plato, what is "just" is to obey the law, which, in turn, was devised for the benefit of those who are "in power." Reference to these shades of meaning regarding man's interdependence will be material for later discussion.

Much later, English philosopher Hobbes (1588–1679) likened the human race to a herd or flock of animals, each of which has its own leader who provides for the needs of the followers.

By supplying pasture and water, the shepherd serves his own needs for, eventually, his welfare depends upon the health and survival of the animals, which he will either trade or devour himself. Nonetheless, the nature and behavior of the husbandman must be more farseeing and compassionate, more honorable and trustworthy than that of the herd that he oversees. Likewise, the leader of a nation must possess surpassing qualities and be of greater nobility than his or her subjects should he or she deserve the right to continue as the designated head of that group of nationals.

For ten years, from AD 31 to AD 41, Caligula was the king and absolute ruler of the Roman Empire. His belief was that earthly kings are like gods and that the people, his subjects, were like the animals of a herd, obliged to follow wherever they are directed. It was his wish that all Roman colonies might be under one head so that with one swing of his sword, he might destroy them all, were that his inclination.

For our purposes, our concluding decision must side with the philosophy of Abraham Lincoln, which, as was stated, maintained that all individuals are created equal and most decidedly must disagree with the attitudes of those philosophers and persons mentioned who suggested that equality is not a characteristic of each human being at the time of creation. And even though all individuals eventually develop great differences from the point of view of language, morality, religious belief, political dogma, and cultural proclivities, there is the need of all—that elusive something for which each is searching—for freedom and for prosperity.

Chapter Two

The Ugly, Grievous War

It now becomes of interest to turn our consideration toward some aspects of our present-day situation and principally to analyze the situation with regard to the conflict surrounding Iraq and Afghanistan. Many wars have been fought in the name of God and of freedom; unfortunately, in such instances, there is always collateral damage, resulting in the deaths of many innocent elderly individuals, women, and children. The tragic events of 9/11, of Jordan, of Madrid, of London, of Bombay, as well as of the daily slaughter in Iraq and some other places have been perpetrated by Middle Eastern extremists, often laboring in the conviction that what they are doing is performed "in the name of God." The retaliatory battles in Afghanistan and Iraq were initiated by Western powers (NATO in the former, U.S. and coalition forces in the latter) and were launched in the name of freedom and democratization. Ironically, one group, al Qaeda, is guilty of a barbarity "in behalf of God" (who, as we have stated at the outset, has no needs) while the opposing Western forces are embattled for freedom's sake (when it is generally understood that the imposition of freedom by force is a tainted independence).

Let us restate this circumstance slightly differently. The killing of nearly three thousand innocent individuals in New York City on 9/11 provoked the United States to react strongly by a declaration of war against those whom it was felt perpetrated that act, namely, the al Qaeda. USA and some of its allies (Great Britain, most notably), the strongest military powers in the modern world, declared war against Osama bin Laden, the leader of the terrorist group al Qaeda.

It is significant to recall that Osama bin Laden had been set up in Afghanistan for a very specific reason. In the first place, he and his Islamic followers were trained to fight the former Communist Soviet Union, who had launched an invasion of Afghanistan. Following the retreat of the Russian Communist forces, an Islamic regime was established in Afghanistan, the Sunni Taliban, which fully supported Osama bin Laden inasmuch as he had offered a significant resistance to the Russians.

Interestingly, the Taliban was recognized only by Pakistan and several other Islamic countries, and it had very hostile relations with the Shiite Islamic regime of Iran. The situation worsened considerably when the Taliban captured eleven Iranian diplomats and executed them by beheading them in the Afghan capitol of Kabul. The major opposition to the Khomeini regime was Saddam Hussein, the Taliban, and the majority of the intellectuals of Iran itself.

Ironically, the Western powers have contributed in a major way to disassemble each of these opponents although in the case of Iraq and Afghanistan, they have accomplished very little after more than four years of outright battle in these nations in the way of diminishing the strength of the terrorist elements. Interestingly, U.S. and European opposition to Iran's possession of "enriched" uranium has also forced Iranian intellectuals into closer alliance with their oppressive regime for the intelligentsia also feel that Iran deserves to possess the refined material—but for peaceful purposes. And unfortunately, the reputation of the United States, once respected as the most powerful military force and enemy of Communism, has deteriorated considerably not only in the Middle East, but also throughout the world because of its unilateral approach to Iraq. Its preeminence during the period of the Cold War, when it employed peaceful means rather than military force in order to encourage freedom and human rights, has diminished significantly.

Middle Easterners (and Europeans alike) much preferred the posture of Uncle Sam as an educator, smuggler of Bibles, and supporter of missionaries rather than as a juggernaut with bombs and Humvees.

This situation poses a serious question. Inasmuch as it is seemingly impossible for the Western powers to achieve a meaningful victory against the elements of terrorism through imposition of military force, is there any way that this problem can be solved? Is there an honorable means whereby a victorious outcome may be achieved? If so, what would that process involve?

To answer these questions, we must turn to really unbiased information. It is necessary to determine the root cause of the dilemma, and after comprehensive examination of this basic information, we may actually strive to discover a permanent understanding and solution to disentanglement of this modern-day cultural snarl.

What Is the Root?

It is my well-grounded theory that at the heart of the ugly war between the West and al Qaeda are two related phenomena: (1) the presence of oil in the Middle East and (2) the establishment of the new State of Israel in the Middle East in 1948. A brief historical review will prove helpful.

In 1899, the French archeologist Jacques de Morgan first sniffed the aroma of oil in Northern Iran, but his scientific colleagues in France were not so advanced in the technicalities of accessing this resource as were the English. So it fell to the lot of his English friend Edward Court in this group of archeologists to sense and to act upon the importance of this discovery. When the men returned to their respective European countries, Edward reported this finding to a business cabal that was engaged in searching for petroleum. They, indeed, were most interested and dispatched representative William Knox d'Arcy to Tehran in 1901. Following numerous appropriate discussions and explanations of his interest to Iranian officials, d'Arcy offered twenty thousand pounds to the government of Iran in order to carry out exploration for oil as well as additional conditions for the extraction of that commodity should results be positive.

After successful search and discovery, d'Arcy won permission to continue drilling for oil for the next sixty years and to share 16 percent of revenues with Iran while deposing the 84 percent remainder less expenses with his English concern. These fiscal conditions remained in force until 1933. Thus, William d'Arcy was the original British explorer and entrepreneur for England in the development of oil trade with Iran.

All proceeded without a hitch until 1933 when the Iranian government summoned d'Arcy and disclosed their displeasure with the arrangements that were in effect inasmuch as this agreement lacked the approval of the Iranian Parliament, which had come into existence in 1906 when Iran had been transformed from a dictatorship into a constitutional monarchy very much like that of England. The Iranian contention was that the old agreement could no longer be honored and was unacceptable without the approval of its representative legislature. D'Arcy very wisely recognized the validity of this argument. A new agreement was drawn up in which Iran was to receive 20 percent of the oil trade profits while d'Arcy and company were entitled to 80 percent minus costs.

Another small alteration had occurred in 1914 when the English government, under Winston Churchill's rule as prime minister, had bought out d'Arcy and company's share of the enterprise and had had all of England's naval ships converted from coal to oil so as to take advantage of this new mercantile asset. This marked the very beginning of the use of oil as an international resource in the struggle to attain wealth and power. And from this point on in history, there arose increasing competition on a global scale for the control of Middle Eastern oil reserves by the world powers, particularly between Russia and England initially but later on between all of the major colonial contenders on the world scene. And recall, it all started in Iran!

For many years, therefore, Iran was held at bay and treated as a pawn in its dealings with West and East (mainly England and Russia, respectively). The once proud Persia was denigrated and adversely affected by its financial and political dealings with the outside world. At one time, there was even a clandestine effort afoot to divide the Iranian territory into a northern portion to be overseen by Russia and a southern part to be controlled by England. However, in 1921, an elite Iranian national, Reza Shah, made a coup d'etat and came into power in his native country as the shah of Iran. He favored Germany and, in turn, was supported by that Western nation. Iran remained as somewhat under the influence of England until it was learned in 1941 that Reza Shah had secretly cooperated with Adolf Hitler—Germans built a railroad from south of Iran to the north, and Hitler also promised to return provinces seized earlier by Russia to his control. England fully realized that Iranian oil and its geographic strategy would help Hitler to get India and Afghanistan, thus immediately responded by having the shah resign and be banned to the South African island of Maoris. The situation remained somewhat vacuous until 1953 when the Soviet-backed Communist Party and Dr. Mohammad Mossadegh seized control of Iran through another coup d'etat and forced Reza Shah's son, Mohammad, to flee penniless to Italy while he, Mossadegh, declared himself president of Iran, disbanded the Parliament and the Senate, and took control of the nation. This new set of circumstances triggered a contrived Western plan (the Ajax plan), which was carried out under the direction of Kermit Roosevelt, the CIA representative of the United States in the Middle East. The result was the downfall of Mossadegh through another coup d'etat led by Iranian royalist officer Zahedi, who was backed by the "plan" and the return of Mohammad Reza Shah Pahlavi to the leadership of Iran once again, all for the expenditure of seventy thousand dollars. Ayatollah Haji shaik Nasrollah Khalkhali, who was the special accountant of the distinguished Islamic spiritual leaders, told me that it is interesting that twenty thousand dollars of seventy thousand dollars has been paid for two famous Ayatollahs: (1) Kashani, he was Mossadegh's peer or close friend; and (2) Borugerdi, as leader of Shiite religion, had a big share in this matter. The question is that since this coup d'etat was encouraged and approved by these two highest ranking of Iranian religious leaders, how could this coup d'etat be illegal according to the Islamic Shiite law? However, all of this intrigue, the international subterfuge and the repeated coup d'etats, resulted in the death of many innocent Iranian nationals in the process. And the concomitant disruption of educational, religious, and cultural activities can never be fully estimated nor understood. Greed and illicit manipulation have devastated the once proud existence of a sovereign people and nation. There remained only the addition of insult to injury to take place: the insertion of the Khomeini regime in 1979 by the oil interests, an event that utterly destroyed the small remaining reputation, culture, dignity, and economy of Iran. This final blow to our heritage is treated in my first book, *A Letter to Intellectuals*.

The irony of all this can be brought out more starkly by this metaphoric illustration: Little Bobbie fell down into his aunt's well in Texas. Rescuers rushed to try to save him, and the media captured this event on TV for all the world to watch. Recall the empathetic global rejoicing that took place on the fifth day of that widely observed event in Texas when little Bobbie was hauled up alive and whole from that well. Unfortunately, more than seventy million Iranians through the years fell into oil wells without anyone to observe nor rescue them. Indeed, the people of Iran then and now have been thirsting for "rescue" and for true freedom and democracy and for relief from the anachronistic Bedouin suppression under which they are still living in this twenty-first century! Sadly, there has been no media nor political agenda to disclose and reveal the fate of all these fallen ones, neither historically nor currently! But reliance upon military force to correct this present ironic situation will never allow for a real victory. We must, rather, comprehend the root of the problem in order to grapple successfully with the evil that has come to pass.

The Root of the Problems

Further, to shed light upon how such a brutal circumstance as the tragedy of 9/11 in New York City could have happened, ask yourself, did the event take place because George W. Bush was president? Or did the origin of the horrendous scheme occur because of provocation at a much earlier date?

As already suggested, there is little doubt in many minds that the idea had its inception in 1948 at the time of the imposition of the new State of Israel in the Middle East as well as in the year 1901 when archeologists first smelled oil in Iran.

It is essential at this point to hear the answer of a Middle Easterner to this question and possibly thereby to gain a little insight into the development of a philosophy like that of al Qaeda.

In suggesting this, I do not mean to imply that Iran has any relations with this organization nor with any other terrorist group nor do I; but since I have lived in the Middle East for over fifty years and since I have heard so many comments and opinions of ordinary people living in that part of the world, I believe that I have gained insight into the attitudes and considerations of individuals who represent that area of our globe. Also, when I worked in the Iranian Intelligence Service, it was my job to listen to and try to analyze the topics of conversation of both ordinary Muslims and Arab politicians. So I have become quite familiar with their drift as they discuss matters of global significance.

As regards the creation of the State of Israel in 1948, a typical Middle Easterner believes that the Western nations brought more than six million Jewish persons from Russia, Europe, and America to Palestine, thereby displacing the rightful owners of the land there and causing many millions of Palestinians to become homeless. Also, in the displacement process, many of the Palestinian refugees were killed. This situation reflects unfavorably upon the involved Western countries and seems to demonstrate an attitude of ingratitude on their part, especially as the uprooting of fellow Arabs followed in the face of years of these Western nations having accrued great wealth from the trade in oil with the surrounding Arab countries. The unconditional support for this new renegade Jewish state flies in the face of decency and lays bare the long-standing excesses of the West at the expense of Middle Eastern culture.

And what is the attitude of these same Middle Easterners toward the Jewish nation itself? They sense that the Israelis receive vast sums of money and unconditional support from many Western countries, especially the United States. It is also regretted that the Israelis have no qualms about killing Palestinian women and children on a daily basis in behalf of protection of their sovereign nation. And Israel is seen as a military power that has so much more than the hapless Palestinians who have nothing that it is not difficult to imagine why an ordinary person like Osama bin Laden, rather than a political bigwig, might conceive the notion of organizing a force counter to the Israel juggernaut, such as that which al Qaeda represents.

In Arab culture, revenge is second nature. The Koran certainly promotes this characteristic: "Va lakom fel hayate kesason ya ollel albab" (translated "You, as wise people, have the right in your lifetime to revenge a misdeed"). Although the governments of several Islamic countries formerly recognized the State of Israel, the populace of those countries most emphatically did not; for deep within their hearts, they had not one iota of compassion for such a rogue state. Control of those countries was in the hands of puppets who, in their feigned allegiance to the will of the United States, carried their tails between their hind legs in order to maintain acceptance in Western diplomatic circles. Proof of the dichotomy between the sentiment of the people of those Arabic countries and the political expression of their leaders is the fact that most of the terrorists who took part in the catastrophe of 9/11 were either from Egypt or Saudi Arabia—only Egypt recognized Israel (the head of the government of the Saudi Arabian kingdom has even been a guest in the Bush home in Texas and claims to be a close friend of the U.S. president). Closest to the truth is that even the heads of these countries, in their real hearts, see Israel as an intruding and illegitimate government in the Middle Eastern region; and they are biding their time until the day when they are strong enough to declare war upon Israel and destroy it!

It is necessary to emphasize, however, that the situation in Iran regarding Israel is really unique for there, the general population does not hate Israel nor the United States in spite of recognized injustices relative to Iran committed by the West in the past. With the exception of Islamic fanatics who are brainwashed by the present anachronistic autocracy that controls Iran, the majority of Iranians are not anti-Semitics at all. Many of them recall Cyrus, the first Persian emperor (550 BC), who granted all citizens in his entire empire a complete listing of human rights, including freedom of religion. At that time, captive Jewish slaves in Babylonia were included in this amnestic policy and were allowed not only religious freedom, but also the right to return to their homeland of Judah in order to rebuild their temple of worship. Indeed, there absolutely is no conflict whatsoever between ordinary, average present-day Iranian citizens and their Israeli counterparts. Harmony with the West is quietly yearned for! And that is in spite of the fact that Western powers actually were responsible for bringing the current reprehensible regime into power—a form of punishment of Iran that intellectuals everywhere deeply regret.

A result of this imposition of a corrupt dictatorship is the fact that four million educated Iranians have dispersed themselves in exile throughout the world inasmuch they could not tolerate the injustices brought about by this infamous tyrannical theocracy. (Please refer to my explanation of this circumstance in the book *A Letter to Intellectuals*.)

The current president of Iran, Mahmoud Ahmadinejad, who carries on the illicit regime of Ali Khamene'i, summarized the Arabic belief concerning Israel well when he said, "Israel must be wiped out, obliterated from the map of the world!" To the Iranian intellectual, he apes "Ahmedi" Khamene'i, and is Boze Akfash, which means he repeats all that Khamene'i says and is one who does not understand the meaning of what he says (he merely pays lip service and agrees without any personal comprehension). In Farsi, the saying is "Pull the goat's beard (goatee), and he answers every question with *baa*." In keeping with what we have just explained then, the utterance of the president is entirely counter to what intellectuals and the average Iranian earnestly feels.

In attempting to expand upon the Arab mind-set as it regards Israel, I am reminded of the occasion in 1966–1971 when I left Tehran and went to Dubai on a special mission. I was also teaching there in Dubai at the Teachers' College. I was living in a rented apartment and had as a neighbor a man from Saudi Arabia. He was a teacher in the school of religion. His name was Abdul-Montakem, which means "servant of a revenger god." He had sight only in one eye. On occasion, we would greet each other. Once, when he had been on a winter vacation and flew back to Shiraz, he noted snow everywhere. Afraid of the cold, he flew farther on to Bandar Abbas, which is much warmer and is not far from Dubai in the Persian Gulf. He called and invited me to his house. While he talked about his vocation in Iran,

I learned of his difficulty with the Iranian language. Since he spoke no Farsi, when he tried to ask for milk for his breakfast, the waiter could not understand him. He, therefore, tried acting out the milking of a cow and eventually made himself understood. Moving on from this lighter and more humorous conversation, he proceeded to share his views of Iranian religion with me. His first comment was that Iranians must not believe in Allah because they say "Ya Ali" or "Ya Hossien," instead of saying "Ya Allah" as do Arabs because "Allah" is God. "Since 'Ali' is like me, Abdul Montakem, and I am not God, they must not believe in God." Understanding his confusion and seeing his point, his simplistic reasoning, somewhat like all Arabs and Sunnis who believe Shiites are not Muslim and, therefore, should be killed.

He then moved the conversation to politics and stated that Iran and Israel are brothers because they are both pro-American! Of course, I was immediately prompted to inquire, "What makes you so sure about that?"

His reply was, "They both have received Black Hawks, helicopters, and F-16s from the USA, which no other countries have. And they are both enemies of us Arabs!" With that, he began to curse and employ such foul language that I became frightened and actually feared for my life. Such simplistic and erroneous reasoning confounded me.

He continued and said that the United States is a colony of Israel because its leaders blindly support that country, which is the Arabs' enemy. He added that revenge is in the blood of every Arab so that someday, the United States and other Western countries will receive their due punishment from the Arabian people.

It is this circuitous, hateful type of thinking that is characteristic of most ordinary Arabs in their general population and with few exceptions. And it is out of this mind-set that Osama bin Laden and members of al Qaeda and the Taliban may trace their allegiance to suicidal revenge upon representatives of Western countries. The dilemma is, How may we alleviate this awful state of affairs with which we are so closely linked as to cause and inception?

One essential to point out before we launch into the text of this book: there was absolutely no al Qaeda, Hezbollah, nor Hamas prior to 1979. The Islamic extremists lacked any cohesive force prior to that time. But with the seeming defeat in Iran of the West and the shah, despite the fact that this overthrow was actually engineered by the Western powers and with the ending of the invasion by Russia of Afghanistan also largely abetted by the West, Islamic fanatical people began to think to themselves, "Hey! We kicked the butt of the shah and his U.S. allies in Iran, and we eliminated Russia from its attempt to seize Afghanistan. Why should we bow down to these foreign cronies anywhere else in our region? Let us organize and show the world that we can be our own bosses!" And so were the inception of al Qaeda, Hezbollah, Hamas, and the terrorist ambiance that characterizes our global situation today.

Chapter Three

The Root of Ideology Schools and Religions vs. Democracy and Science

1. Reload

The primary need of human kind is a continuous awareness of knowledge (or wisdom) from the time of infancy to the time of death.

Philosophers, scientists, intellectuals, prophets, and religious leaders each have different points of view concerning awareness of what a god is, what humankind is, what the universe is, as well as what is good and what is bad.

There is no doubt that the very first basic human need is the desire to know answers to their problems. Indeed, human beings are always searching to understand themselves, God, good and bad, and the universe from the very beginning of time to the present. The greatest philosophers and scientists in times past and present have written volumes upon these matters—Aristotle, Socrates, Plato, Confucius, Vedas, Buddha, Kant, Mill, Rousseau, and Russell are only a small sampling of the many through the ages who have explored truth and searched for facts without imposing their own personal feelings and religious beliefs that might distort reality. Their utmost desire was to know what comprises the universe, what the purpose of life is, what God is, and what is good and what is bad.

2. Ideology: Philosophers and Religions

A pupil of Kant, German philosopher Fichte (1814) believed the picture of a thing is the truth about an object for how one sees a thing in one's brain is more real than the object itself as it exists in physical form. The actuality of an object is that which is pictured or captured in your brain; and the phenomena of touch, sound, smell, or sight of an object are lesser realities. According to Fichte, the actual physical existence of an object (a pen, for instance) is not a fact, but the picture captured in one's brain of that object (pen) is really the true fact.

Another German philosopher, Schelling (1854), had an opposite point of view, namely, that the true fact is the exterior actuality of an object and not the picture of that object captured in the brain. The famous Hegel, another noted German philosopher (1831), endorsed the argument of Fichte with very outspoken statements. These two German philosophers were considered idealists and contributed significantly to some of the basic ideological reasoning of Nazi Fascists, Russian Communists, and religious idealism like Judaism and Islam even though these entities are antagonistic and contradict one another in their teaching, regardless of their common root.

In the Communist tradition, it is maintained that the individual (leader or follower) has no inherent worth, so an individual must correctly sacrifice himself or herself for the greater good so as to assist the more important cause of society. Whereas, in Fascist reasoning, within the party itself, the individual has great importance as contrasted to the person outside the party who is of no value and may easily be destroyed. And in the Fascist scheme of society, leadership is akin to godliness, and party members must be willing to sacrifice themselves in behalf of the one who is leader. In Islam, there are rewards for such self-destruction, and happiness and leisure are achieved in life after death as compensation for suffering for the head of the party. Self-denigration to enhance the place and needs of the leader are the privileges of party membership.

Deprivation of worldly pleasure for the advancement of the leadership are the signs quinine of Fascist ideology. The ideal party member is willing to tolerate all manner of torture, beating, and deprivation in deference to the religiously imposed command of the chief!

And exploration into truth as it exists in the real world outside of the party is strictly forbidden.

Should a subject wander outside the prescribed paths and happen upon a truth in opposition to the leadership, then a death sentence may very likely be imposed.

We are reminded of the death sentence imposed upon S. Rushdie for his book *Satanic Verses*. The Islamic regime currently ruling Iran (and Fascist in kind) is solemn in nature and has offered six million dollars to anyone who kills him. And a Dutch cartoonist has a million-dollar bounty on his head even though his own country found him not guilty of wrongdoing. Pope Benedict

XVI, in a public speech, spoke supportively of the fourteenth-century Roman emperor who deplored Mohammedanism as vengeful and was reprimanded by all Muslims with general retribution threatened toward all Christians. Thinking outside of the box is so restricted in countries subject to Fascist control, as is present-day Iran, that its people have little opportunity to experience prosperity, peace of mind, and happiness; and a hateful ambiance stifles freedom at every turn.

At the opposite spectrum of social infrastructure lies the predominant philosophy of John Stuart Mill, a famous English thinker, also of the nineteenth century, who promulgated a capitalistic or capitalistic social democratic theory and individual liberty. When viewed next to the enlightened thinking of this philosophical giant, the regressive social attitudes of Fascism and Communism must be adjudged as wrong and injurious to any group of people aspiring to progress in technology, fiscal growth, or constructive social consciousness.

Obeying an innate curiosity, true science involves the exploration for knowledge by means of unbiased research and experimentation. If discoveries are made, conclusions are drawn only according to the insights of such investigation. Progress is achieved on the basis of that which is observable. And this leads us to an understanding of the difference between science and reason versus faith and religion. Knowledge, as extolled by the prophet and religiously inspired individual, depends upon revelation from an invisible source, namely, God. Truth is "heaven-sent."

There is an historic dichotomy between these two lines of reasoning for we easily recall instances of discord between cleric and scientist when an interaction between the two disciplines has occurred. The excommunication of Galileo because of his Copernicus-based insistence that the earth revolved around the sun is certainly an outstanding instance of this sort; agreement was impossible, and for a long while, the church prevailed.

The struggle between science and religion was modified somewhat by efforts of the vigilantes and intellectuals who tried to effect reconciliation amid the various segments of human life. They inferred that human beings must live together in spite of their differences and the impracticability at times of doing so. Moves in this direction can be made only very gradually; and there is no one simple means of rapprochement that will cover differences and still allow provision for the coverage of human needs, including equal rights, avoidance of discrimination, freedom of thought (both individually and groupwise), self-expression, and security from the cradle to the grave. Indeed, rather than the achievement of one comprehensive solution to effect harmony, the acceptance of compromise may only be achieved in small steps with partial surrender of principle on the part of each competing moiety bit by bit. Obstacles to cooperation must be thoroughly weighed, given credence, and then gently erased in order to promote progress. We should not offend any party in a conflict, be it religious or scientific or otherwise, and we must honor all cultural characteristics.

There follows a listing of three events helpful to the communicative process among religion, science, and intellect. First, in 550 BC, Cyrus the Great, the first Persian emperor, created basic foundations for the exercise of human rights throughout his entire empire, thereby opening the way for the dissemination of knowledge, individual creativity, and recognition of the value of the human race.

Secondly, the French Revolution in the eighteenth century was of enormous help in assisting the spread of democracy and freedom of religion, especially in the Western countries, in part because of the simultaneous dawn of the Industrial Revolution and of scientific technology.

There occurred huge progress in many areas of mechanization and communication that assisted the development of social democracies on the North American continent and also in Europe, principally Sweden and Norway. Individual and group creativity were fostered, with people exerting their ingenuity through freedom of self-rule by the opportunity of independent elections. Great progress in education and self-expression were made possible because of the accessibility of the freedom of mind and body, which ideals of freedom are essential for the dissemination and application of methods to help melt barriers and to secure human needs. Such were by-products of the French Revolution.

A third historical stimulus to the harmonizing process affecting religion, science, and intellect was the establishment in the early twentieth century of the League of Nations, supplanted somewhat later by the United Nations. This was a global expression in the process of promoting communication and international cooperation to assist in the spreading of awareness of social problems and the actual meeting of human need worldwide. It also was an attempted major step forward in international peacemaking. Unfortunately, the exercise of veto power became an important detriment to the easy accomplishment of the mission of this ecumenical body.

Although all participating countries were supposed to contribute to the support of this global institution proportionally to the size of their populations, those with veto power mainly determined the direction and application of benefits.

Even though Cyrus the Great provided opportunity for freedom of thought and religion to the Persian people in his day and age, ironically, the population of present-day Iran is suffering from Fascistic religious suffocation at the hands of a theocratic dictatorship that compels the Iranian people to a very miserable sort of life. Also, beneficial effects of the French Revolution could not prevent Western powers from the colonization and manipulative force that subjugated other national economies. The Platonic principle "Might makes right" predominated, however unfairly, in some aspects of international relations.

War is the enemy of many; the poor and downtrodden are among the majority of those who suffer the most. And even "near" war provokes undue hardship for those who are innocent bystanders and are only secondarily involved. Witness the desultory effect of the Cold War and of today's terrorist war. Thousands of ordinary Iraqi citizens have lost their lives in a bloodbath of still undetermined proportions, and such a pity if it all traces back to greed for oil. Recall, we have insinuated that the Muslim terrorists were incited, at least in part by injustices in the management by Western countries of their relations with these Middle Eastern countries through years of petroleum-trade development—colonization and usurious economic arrangements that failed to benefit the hapless possessors of this dark resource. Can we accept our share of blame for this ironic turn of events, complicated by the tragedy of a humongous loss of lives?

If we think about the average human being, we realize that he or she is not very often presented with the opportunity to think about one's destiny in great depth. And relatively few have the privilege of performing scientific experiments. Most are forced to spend their waking hours working to meet the demands for securing daily needs for themselves and their dependents. The encouragement that is provided through the aegis of religious belief satisfies a very natural need for emotional and spiritual support for many in confronting the hardships of the "real" life. And although some beliefs are actually synonymous with unconfirmed yearnings and superstition, those privileged few who are allowed to research more deeply the human comedy and themselves are less likely to be captivated by superstition, decide against upsetting the applecart, and are willing to relegate many sacred "cows" to the realm of custom and folk art—not to be railed against, but rather to be accepted as part of dignified culture and as a rubberneck that makes life more bearable. In short, they use their privileged knowledge and understanding with empathy and dedicate their investigative efforts not to tear down and demean, but rather to bolster and to more easily insinuate progress into the fabric of civilization and culture. Rather than inflame and abrade, these scientists and intellectuals prefer to adorn and enhance culture, thereby contributing their knowledge to solution rather than to confounding of human problems—a knowledge basic to a focus on the needs of all humans on this planet.

Basic to all religious beliefs is a need for law and order; a mode of operation that will undergird management of the family, the tribe (community), or nation. This is an overarching system of behavior, a "superior law" that must be complied to in addition to the day-to-day operational principles that guide the function of society—simpler rules, which, if disobeyed, result in fine or punishment. It is a standard of personal responsibility to which every knee is willing to bend in order for society to flourish and benefit, a subscribed-to norm that is innate and not enforced from without. In short, it is the accepted way of life, and it permits an equitable existence when if is framed with love or one that is steeped with injustice when not so blessed.

A government based upon democratic philosophy and freedom implies a rule in which each individual is important and happily self-disciplined. Let us refer to this sort of regime as a capitalistic or capitalistic social democracy. In it are guaranteed freedom of religion, thought, speech, and pursuit of happiness. Personal welfare, health, and social equity are assured privileges through the function of governmental, church, and civic activities. Appropriate agencies assist in the securing of these civil rights.

Whereas a government based on idealistic philosophy and submission implies a regime in which each individual is regarded as a subject and requires control, we refer to this sort of government as Social Communism or Fascist Nationalism. Again, the former Soviet Union and Nazi Germany, respectively, are foremost examples of such ideologies while the present dictatorial Islamic hagiarchy in Iran is a reflection of the Hitler regime. Such governments cannot afford the freedoms allowed in the democracies described in the preceding paragraph, and because they do not function for the benefit of individual members of their citizenry who live in subjugation, civil rights are nonexistent.

Because there are so many different beliefs in the world, a standard of behavior is a very diverse element. Usually, each culture teaches that true happiness and prosperity derive only from its own set of beliefs. It is even argued that other cultures are wrong and that adherents to such a culture are lost or, at the least, unfortunate. At the extreme, moreover, it may even be argued that followers of a different culture are better off to be gotten rid of, or destroyed, especially if elements of their beliefs are contrary to one's own. A more moderate attitude, and one that would be more anthropologically sound and realistic, would be that one's cultural beliefs are correct or better than another but that "others" must be reckoned with and honored and its adherents must be treated with respect.

Let it not remain unsaid that there are some religious leaders who would misrepresent and exaggerate their feelings that their ideas deserve primacy and would misappropriate and misapply the idiom "in the name of God" whereas God is holy, pure, and clean, and hardly fits into the pronouncements with which such "holy" shepherds seek to deceive their naive flock, even to the point of commission of absolutely horrendous crimes, and for the purpose of establishing an authority that is most certainly undeserved. Indeed, some very intelligent, shrewd, and near-genius individuals have in the past and continue in the present to misdirect and abuse the energies of simple and unsuspecting folk in crusades fabricated "for the glory of God" and "in the name of God"!

Similarly, many politicians in the past, as well the present, misuse the religious beliefs of people for the purpose of gaining governance over them in order to maintain and enhance their power. These political opportunists claim their authority through the guise of democracy but are, in fact, dictators who claim their authority in the name of God. They usurp freedom, property, and the rights of their subjects. Often, in the process, many innocent human beings lose their very lives as sacrifices to the capricious whims and the personal greed of these power-thirsty miscreants. Especially prone to the unjust ravages of such despots are innocent elderly, widows, and orphans. Thousands upon thousands in the twentieth or twenty-first century have lost parents and family brother or sister breadwinners or have been incapacitated explicitly due to the injustices committed by such egotistic heads of government.

Examples of the tragic situations alluded to in the preceding paragraph include (1) daily massacres by insurgency of senior citizens and other innocent men, women, and children in Iraq and Afghanistan; (2) daily killings in Palestine by Israel, using cluster bombs in residential areas of Palestine and Lebanon; (3) slaying of citizens of Israel by Hezbollah using Ketusha rockets; (4) bombings by al Qaeda in London, Jordan, Oman, Madrid, and Tunisia; (5) inhumane torture by the U.S. military (usually by small groups of aberrant individuals acting without proper control and dominated by a destructive "mass psychology") at Abu Ghraib, Guantanamo, and certain Iraqi locations; (6) the tragedy of 9/11 fomented by Osama bin Laden; (7) the coup d'etat backed by big oil companies in Iran that allowed the establishment of a regressive Islamic regime that has destroyed its economy and status as a global entity; (8) establishment in 1948 of the current nation of Israel in Palestine by major power agreement (primarily, the United Nations) with resulting refugee status of millions of Palestinians; (9) the division following the Second World War by allies of certain countries (e.g., Germany) that resulted in a divisive splitting of control under either East or West; and (10) the Cold War between East and West initiated by oil interests in Iran and stemming from the Tehran Conference.

The final item above requires some explanatory discussion. Between November 29 and December 2, 1943, Joseph Stalin of Russia, Winston Churchill of Great Britain, and President Franklin Roosevelt of the United States—the major representatives of the allies—were in conference in Tehran to deal with the outcome of the Second World War. They expressed appreciation for the strategic military importance of Iran and gave assurance to that nation, describing it as "the bridge of victory." The Allied powers further promised to honor the territorial integrity of Iran; Russia and England indicated that they were committed to withdrawing their troops from Iran at the conclusion of the war, and the three major powers promised to reimburse Iran for expenses incurred by the Iranian government for food and lodging supplied to occupation forces of the Allies during the war. In October 1944, a U.S. minister came to Iran for the first time to secure concession of oil to the United States. He was welcomed, and concession was made. From prewar understanding, England already enjoyed oil rights in the southern region of Iran. To bolster its position in the northern part of Iran and to ensure access to oil there, Russia also sent a minister (Caftar Zadah) to Iran at this time. However, as a result of some ongoing unpleasant relations with USSR, the requests of the Soviet envoy were heard; but no definite concessions were made by the Iranian government. This deeply disturbed Joseph Stalin, so at the conclusion of the war in Europe, USSR did not withdraw its troops from Northern Iran. Stalin contended that it was wrong that the United States, ten thousand miles from Iran, and England, five thousand miles away, were party to oil from Iran while neighboring Russia, with a long border with Iran, was denied any share in that precious resource.* Furthermore, Stalin then assisted the Communist Party of Iran (Tudah) and Jaffar Pishah Vari to establish a portion of the northern territory of Iran as the independent republic of Azerbaijan with Pishavari as its imposed president. Under this newly instigated political pressure, Iran then ceded half of the huge oil reserves in the Caspian Sea region to the Soviet Union, following which was a concession where the USSR withdrew its troops from its northern territory and gave a part of Azerbaijan back to Iran.

In fairness to the countries involved in the "reimbursement" aspect of the Tehran Agreement in 1945, Russia gave eleven tons of gold and eighteen million dollars to Iran in payment for World War II troop costs while the United States returned eighteen gold bullion and England several gold bullion to compensate for military lodging expenses incurred by Iran.

Certain other promises made to Russia by the Iranian prime minister were later rejected by Iran's parliament, further illustrating the somewhat unsavory relationship of the two countries at that time. Russia then reannexed Iran's portion of Azerbaijan as a republic of the USSR, disregarding its agreement at the Tehran Conference regarding respect for the integrity of Iran, and this initiated the phase of global history known as the Cold War. Of course, the rich oil reserves of northeastern Azerbaijan were already the property of USSR, which circumstance had been a sizeable loss for Iran and further illustrates the argument that OIL WAS, IN REALITY, THE BASIS FOR THE COLD WAR.

After the Iranian Oil Company was nationalized in 1954, the nation of Iran formalized the disposition of its oil resources as follows: One half of its daily output of between four and six million barrels per day were distributed—40 percent each to England and the United States, and 5 percent each to Holland and France. Each country agreed to pay 50 percent of the money earned from its share of this oil to Iran while keeping the other 50 percent of sale profit for itself. In essence, one-half of the oil sales was for the benefit of the outside countries and one-half for its provider, the country of Iran. This apportionment of oil was in effect for twenty years or until the '79 revolution.

The above incidents contributing to much misery and degradation are mentioned only briefly at this time to cite examples of events resulting in the plundering of the wealth of countries and their populace beyond the imaginations of most of us. Were we to add up the expenses invoked by these occurrences, the sum total would exceed trillions, perhaps quadrillions of dollars—a portion of which, had it been applied to the relief of the needy of the world, would have resulted in the elimination of hunger today in Darfur, any of many places in Africa, or in any place in the world. All the destitute of the world would have benefitted well beyond our fondest conjecture, and peace and the fruits of love would have held sway! And recall that most of these criminal events took place with some party or parties believing that what was transpiring was "in the name of God" or for the sake of a greater freedom.

It was Socrates in 429 BC who likened the individuals or groups of persons perpetrating these calamities to a mythical monster with a tail borrowed from a dragon, half of its body that of a goat and the other half of a furious lion, and maintained the face of a human being. Such creatures promote injustice and disharmony in the name of justice. A name for this sort of horrible monster is Chimera, and according to Socrates, its personality is totally devoid of knowledge or understanding.

As we conjecture about the root of the present conflict confronting us as "east" and "west," epitomized with the term "terrorism," we recognize the countless number of innocent civilians as well as military personnel suffering death and maiming and the tragic loss of children, spouses, and parents, with the resulting needless upheaval of family tranquility and identity.

What possible solution may we come upon to modify and even to terminate this pathos?

Human needs never end and often are impossible to contemplate. They cause people to struggle endlessly for survival and even to make war with one another. And greed ostensibly is the motivation for such conflict. For example, large Western oil companies take advantage of the backwardness of Eastern colleagues and strive to squeeze cheap oil from their reserves of that commodity. Greed is the motivation for conspiracy, fomenting of coup d'etat and intrigue known as political gaming. A great deal of information in this regard has been provided by Harvard University professor Dr. Daniel Yergin in his book entitled *Oil, Power, and Money.*

And further insight may be gained by reference to my first book, *A Letter to Intellectuals.* As I have explained, it certainly was for the sake of this black gold that the oil companies imposed such a backward group of mullahs upon the people of Iran in order to stifle any possible progress that the country might make in science and technology.

As individuals and nations progress, their needs escalate. Often, they are required to make simultaneous choices, to make peace with allies and to fight with enemies. Much of the motivational energy for the establishment of centers of higher learning derives from a basic drive for power and authority as is also true for many projects devoted to exploration and scientific research. Even if we understand as fully as possible all aspects of our planet—geological, oceanic, spatial—we have not yet achieved enough knowledge to enable us to live forever.

As advanced as we believe that we are here in the twenty-first century, we have probably learned only .25 percent of the information that it is necessary to know in order for us to extend our lives considerably, and there is 99.75 percent more information to be gleaned before we have sufficient understanding to carry on our lives forever.

Years ago, the average length of life was thirty to forty years; with increased knowledge and insight into management of life processes, the span of life increased to forty to fifty years. With the passage of time and increased medical and nutritional know-how, the average length of life in the United States and Europe today has increased to seventy to eighty years. And it is possible in this process of reasoning to imagine extending life spans toward an infinity of years! A tenth-century Iranian philosopher, Ghazali, believed that if scientists of the world could fully comprehend their human nature, then they would solve all the mysteries of the world.

Each human being on this planet requires not only to satisfy physical needs but also to meet intellectual hunger in order to communicate and cooperate—whatever the differences in race, language, culture, and religious belief—with his fellow beings. All are like the one human body of which we wrote earlier with its seventy trillion interdependent cells that require shared nutrition, communication, and symbiosis in order to remain healthy and to resist infection, debility, and neoplasia. Without this sharing, sickness and death would ensue. If distrust, intrigue, and deception replace peaceful coexistence, then destruction of the individual occurs like a fatal illness, and life becomes impossible.

If we examine in depth the current struggle between East and West, it becomes clear that there is no victory possible for either side. The Western side leans heavily upon military might and refined technology in order to subjugate its enemy while the Eastern counterparts implore religious idealism and hope for a better future to blast its opponent. Mutual destruction is the result. Nescience prevails, and innocent lives failing to realize their glorious inborn potential are snuffed out on both sides—revenge as a human motif rather than bowing down to the moral truth that "vengeance is the Lord's." One cannot effect a cure without a panacea of love.

The action of the al Qaeda insurgents in Iraq echoes the irony of the Iranian poet who described the wrongdoings of an ironworker in Balkh,* compensated by the killing of a goldsmith in Baghdad without their being the slightest relationship between the two individuals. This is not unlike the tragic recent incident in Pennsylvania when a mixed-up man of forty years justified the killing of five innocent young Amish girls and then of himself because he had been abused by some woman twenty years earlier, and it is also like the taking by air of 3,500 lives in New York City on 9/11 because of the establishment of the nation of Israel with air power supplied by the West in 1948.

I reiterate: In my opinion, there is no true victory possible for either party in our present war with terrorism. And even if there were to be a semblance of victory for either party, it would only be temporary for a permanent victory could only be possible with cultural understanding that would demand an awareness, with cooperation and communication between the two warring factions.

---

* Balkh is a city in Northwestern Afghanistan in the province of Mazār-e Sherīf, west of Turkestan.

For example, if we look back on the 1967 war in Israel with the Arabs, after six days of battle, the Israeli forces had achieved a military victory; however, unrest and combat continue today, and one must question if peace and stability will ever be achieved. Psychological and spiritual condescendence by the Arabs has never occurred, and their resistance to Israel goes on.

Similarly, U.S. military power toppled Saddam Hussein in Iraq in a short period of time as well as the Taliban in Afghanistan; but in both countries, the insurgents continue to struggle and to kill both military personnel and hapless Iraqis and Afghans. Even the deaths of enemy leaders, such as Saddam's two sons, and the capture, imprisonment, court trial, and hanging of Saddam and his cabinet as well numerous al Qaeda leaders in Afghanistan have occasioned little change in the intensity of guerilla warfare in either country. The killing of Zarqawi in Iraq and the imprisonment of the brain behind the massive slaughter of 9/11 (Khalid Sheikh Mohammed) has had little effect upon resistance and conflict abroad; and the number of innocents slaughtered daily continues, even increases, on a per diem basis. One must ponder what useful purpose this cycle of events serves.

There is an old story dealing with Mullah Nosro al-Din, who was a famous anecdotal humorist and who was sitting on a healthy branch of a diseased tree. He took an ax to cut off and preserve the branch. Someone came by and questioned what he was doing, pointing out that if he proceeded in this action, he would also fall down. Mullah laughed and ignored the warning. He and the branch tumbled together. On impact, Mullah was injured and called for help. When reminded of the precautionary advice rendered, Mullah refused any blame for his predicament and failed even to see that the now useless healthy branch lay on the ground while the diseased tree remained standing. Like in our current struggle, no useful purpose had been served by the action taken, and even harm had resulted!

My premise again is that the West must identify the root cause of this present conflict. Why did the terrorists choose to plot against the United States rather than some other nation?

At the very moment that I was reconsidering this matter, a seventy-three-year-old lady called me by phone from Iran. She is referred to by Iranians in Farsi as "the mother of Hassan," and she engaged my attention by crying loudly and uttering this oath, "A curse upon oil!" I implored her to explain to me why she was crying and cursing oil. Her sobbing reply was that her son had gone with family and friends to Najaf, Iraq, for a pilgrimage in honor of Ashura, an observance of the slaying of Imam Hussein, which is a special holiday for Shiite Muslims, and had been murdered there with ten other friends by Iraqi insurgents. She punctuated this revelation by repeating, "Hey, oil, a curse on you!" and reechoed this frenzied imprecation by saying, "Hey, oil, you gave all your empowering profits to the West and all of your destructive qualities to the Middle East!" and "Hey, oil, you killed so many innocent civilians and military people on both sides throughout history!" and "Hey, oil, a curse on you for you brought the mullah to control and to occupy the throne of the Keyan dynasty and brought this fate upon us!" And she spat upon the oil and repeated, "Hey, oil, you have impoverished us!" and "Death to you, oil!"

I implored her again to try to take it easy and to be patient, and I prayed, "May God comfort you and those whom you love!"

37

Her sobbing was then maximized in loud cries as she finally hung up the telephone.

In conclusion of this chapter then, I emphasize these points:

Point One

1. The Portuguese came to the Persian Gulf and colonized Bahrain (231 square miles) in AD 1507, famed for pearl fishing. Bahrain is the center of the Persian Gulf and founded Bandar Gombroon (Bandar Abass). It was retaken through battle and defeat of the Portuguese in 1602 by Shah Abass, the Iranian emperor who restored the small territory (Bahrain and Bandar Gombroon) to the motherland Iran and renamed the port Gombroon to his name as Bandar Abass (Port Abass). Following the First World War, England colonized what is present-day Palestine, Iraq, Jordan, Saudi Arabia, and several crucial sheikdoms that had been part of the Persian Empire (today's United Arab Emirates). Qatar (four thousand square miles) and Kuwait (six thousand square miles), both of which had been occupied by the Ottoman Empire and the latter of which lies at the head of the Persian Gulf, were also taken over by England. (Note: both sides of the Persian Gulf belonged to the Persian Empire as its original territories, but weakness and carelessness plus lacking knowledge of central government of Persia permitted the Ottoman Empire and England to colonize the other side of the Persian Gulf.)

Churchill understood clearly that oil was the most profitable commodity and required utmost focus.

England's advanced technology allowed them to perceive that Iran and the Persian Gulf area would be the greatest source of oil in all the world. Because they also realized that they could not keep this area always in their control, they formulated a plan whereby they might be able to ensure that this huge oil resource might continue to benefit them even if the territories should gain independence. The primary endeavor in this behest was to grant liberty to each of the smaller sheikdoms and to appoint in every such area one sheik whose loyalty was understood to be to England only and to no other external power. Further, to ensure the isolation of these territories for England's advantage, no visas were to be granted to foreign visitors; and no treaties nor agreements were to be made regarding military, political, or economic activities with any other national interest.

England also appointed as leader one person (king) to preside over each country, including Iraq, Jordan, and Saudi Arabia. Such an appointee was not necessarily a native of the country whose kingship he assumed. As for Palestine, the English discovered that the Jewish people there held the belief that Canaan had been given to the Hebrews by God and that they were the intended owners of what they described in Yiddish as Eretz Israel. So eventually, England decided to establish in 1948 the new nation of Israel, which was to be a new homeland for Jews from all over the world. In so doing, England fully realized that its own vital oil interests in that region and those of all the West would thereby be protected and maintained by this foot in the door situation. A future guarantee of the much-needed resource of oil was thus provided both to England and the West.

Great Britain also appointed as a king, with a concordant salary, Sheik Khazal to be the head of Khūzestān, a portion of Southern Iran with huge oil reserves, just as had been their custom in other parts of the Middle East. The shah of Iran (Reza Shah), upon learning of this arrangement, reacted to it with a military force, removed the sheik, and had him exiled to Iraq. This event would provoke future repercussions.

2. On the whole, after both the First and the Second World Wars, the Persian Gulf, Iraq, Palestine, Jordan, and almost all of the Arab countries were subject to the colonization of Great Britain and France (as per the Sykes-Picot Agreement drawn up secretly in 1916 between two countries). Solely, Iran was a domain that never experienced the domination of another foreign intruder. Because both the Western powers (primarily England) and the East (predominantly Russia) were aware of the past history of Iran and understood its pride and the pervasiveness of Persian culture, there was no way that they were willing to risk the cost in human life and expenditure of energy necessary to bring that nation directly into submission to their control. Nonetheless, because of the very strategic location of Iran and their desire to exploit its rich oil resources, both West and East constantly plotted and intrigued to keep the nation off balance and, thereby, to influence and to indirectly dominate its present and future.

In so doing, a great deal of harm, indeed a calamity, accrued to Iran—a situation that continues even today. Freedom to the access of knowledge and to the development of technology have ultimately been denied to the Iranian people, which now has become a very sore point in the global relations that Iran emphasizes to the world at the present.

Point Two

An interesting sociological parallel: In 1906, Iran became a constitutional monarchy, as did Norway and Denmark several years later. These Scandinavian countries have since become two of the most democratic countries in the world whereas Iran, due to outside intrigue and interference for purposes of control of oil and manipulation for strategic importance, has been kept from any real democratic progress, with the majority of its population living as in the Dark Ages and in relatively miserable economic and political circumstances. With the present imposed kakistocracy, the situation is intolerable, and one of the most appealing options is the chance to die with the opportunity of glorious approval from Allah! Whence springs terrorism? one asks.

An interesting economic reflection: In France today, three-quarters of its electric power is derived from atomic energy sources, and the country has made an atomic bomb. USA, England, Russia, Pakistan, India, and Israel also have atomic energy; and each has atomic bombs. Germany and Japan have atomic electricity but, as yet, no known atomic bomb. When Iran expressed the desire to develop enriched uranium for a source of energy, all of these nations opposed the undertaking and have sought sanctions against Iran. These nations justified their opposition to Iran's wish by declaring that Iran is controlled by a terrorist regime, that it supports terrorism throughout the world, and that it is radically opposed to the nation of Israel.

The question must be asked at this juncture: who imposed this terrorist regime upon the Iranian nation? Why, indeed, England, France, and the USA, through clandestine means, brought about the imposition of this nefarious authority upon the unsuspecting and innocent people of Iran. There is the irony! The very Western powers that surreptitiously brought about the present unfortunate state of political affairs in my beloved country of Iran now forbid my people to ease their misery by the economic necessity of developing enriched uranium for energy requirements and even threaten punishment for the further pursuit of this technological necessity. Where is the logic and justice in such an international policy?

Let me try further to consider this point. Only a small fanatical religious group was placed

on purpose by the West in a position of power in Iran. Their cultural norms are as much different from those of the people that they rule as is the distance from earth to heaven for Iranian custom is based upon truth, love, and compassion. If we recall what Saadi had to say about the culture of Iran, "Please don't bother an ant that has a piece of grain in its mouth for it is most anxious to possess that piece of grain. That insect is important because life is sweet for everyone—be it human, feral, or insect." There is no such thing as revenge in Persian culture, such is the modus operandi of the Islamic fanatics who exert control over their subjects. Their special police (Pasdar) and secret police (plainclothes man) and the Hezbollah (party of God) are found in every city in possession of power, money, and position of dominance. Every week, these forces recruit huge crowds from villages, towns, and cities far and near by bus, train, and plane without any cost to them for transportation, lodging, and food in order to show the world via TV that these masses of people are full in accord with the illegitimate regime that rules over them and agree in their opposition to the West. But this is not what the masses truly feel. Were they not bribed in this manner, they would never have agreed to acting in this way and followed the directions of their overseer government. And keep in mind that there is a very high rate of unemployment. Most of those who are employed have some connection or reason for loyalty to the illegal government or have secured work through a special connection. The masses that are recruited for propaganda purposes have no choice but to accept the bonuses and bribes offered them for most often that is their only source of income for the time being. In this way, large crowds in every city are gathered every Friday for prayer demonstrations then are shipped back home by their fanatic bosses, only to be shipped to a different city for a similar demonstration the next week. All this to fool and to deceive foreign reporters who are unaware of the shenanigans and the nature of these contrived scenes.

In this way, the impression that most Iranians are anti-West and supportive of the corrupt theocracy ruling over them is distributed all over the world when, in reality, it is my contention that they are not. The actual situation is that present day Iranians are "in jail" under the rule of a dictatorial Islamic regime. Many Western political leaders are aware of these circumstances, but for the sake of control of the regional oil resources and its prices, they are continuously ready to support the imposition of these tyrants called Muslim overseers. This is a wrong assumption by the Western political leaders.

And as for the matter of sanctions, when the USA made economic restrictions against these renegade Iranian dictators, they were indirectly assisting the economies of England, France, Germany, and Russia (and even their own) because these countries will sell their merchandise at a much higher price (double or triple the cost) to Iran under the pretext of sanctions; for these countries indicate that when they do business with Iran, it must be carried out at a much higher expense level so that they may avoid the wrath of superpower USA, who might, in turn, impose sanctions against them for trading with Iran at a more normal cost range.

As to the statement of Iranian president Ahmadinejad that "Israel must be wiped off the face of the earth," it was by such a statement that he finessed the USA and other Western countries into taking the stand to prevent Iran from carrying out the enrichment of uranium. It was also by this outlandish statement that he assisted Israeli lobbyists more easily to procure financial and material aid from their Western allies (especially USA) for their protection. The statement was widely broadcast and placed him in the position of a Hitler although, indeed, he is not in such a position. But Western powers are making him out to be in order to gain their objectives; and Ahmadinejad himself, by such propaganda, is under the illusion that the twelfth Imam has granted him such divine power to assume this powerful role (that of Hitler) in order to frighten the West (USA, Europe, and Israel) and to render them unable to stand up against him!

To resort to such demagoguery is a most serious matter and the worst temptation that a political leader ought to resist. For example, it led to a war between Iran and Iraq for eight years that cost for no real reason the lives of two million of those countries' best young men and, in addition, resulted in the handicapping of many more without hands, legs, or eyesight. And this was done in the expenditure of four hundred billion dollars, again, for no real reason—save to flatter the egos of maniacs like Khomeini and Saddam Hussein. And the USA had a part in the insanity, with Rumsfeld secretly traveling from Washington DC to Baghdad to tell Hussein that we supported him and would assist him with this conflict with Iran while a few years later, Lawrence Rockefeller, chief advisor on U.S. National Security in the Reagan administration, journeyed to Tehran with Oliver North—with a letter, a cake, and a personally autographed Bible from President Reagan in hand to assure Khomeini that the United States would sell weapons to Iran for its part in battling Iraq, such a clandestine adventure in spite of the fact that Congress had passed a law that

Reagan himself had signed that the United States would not supply weapons of any sort to Iran. The deal was climaxed at an extremely high price for Iran, and both Israel and Nicaragua received without cost as a go-between one hundred million dollars each! This covert action eventually was divulged; and for the continued madness that it represented, Oliver North was taken to court and sentenced to three years in jail while Khomeini, under the authority of the two-faced Islamic regime, denied the entire affair and had all the Iranians involved in divulging the matter murdered in the dark of night. So in point of fact, demagoguery is a nefarious game and today leads the Hezbollah-inspired Islamic regime of Iran to direct the innocent Iranian actors to shout, "Death to America and Israel!" while, at the same time, squirreling away the historical truth that dollars and business have transpired with the so-called hated enemies of Allah.

If we look at past history to discover any affront that Iran may have perpetrated against Europe or the USA before the imposed Islamic regime was empowered by the West, we cannot discover any. That Rumsfeld would suggest to Saddam that the United States would support Iraq against Iran and that Germany would provide Saddam with chemical weapons to use against Iran are unjustified political ploys to maintain the enslavement of Iran to the global whims of the world outside of my native land for the irresistible attraction for the rich oil reserves that we possess and that the outside world wishes to access at any cost!

There is not a single incident in world history of provocation by the nation of Iran for such mistreatment by their global peers as I have indicated. On the contrary, Europe and the USA have always benefitted immensely from the huge wealth of Iran, its great resources of oil, and the natural friendliness of its people. Picture the large number of Iranian subjects being abused and tortured by this imposed illegal Muslim regime and liken them, if you can, to the unfortunate innocent people who were victimized on 9/11 and who were helpless in the face of the horrendous attack carried out during that tragic event. Unfortunately, the irony and truth of the situation is that the thoughtless and inhumane policies of the governments of the Western powers have allowed the development of the conditions that have led to terroristic attitudes and psychologies that now trouble our modern world.

There is a Persian proverb that says that someone may do a good thing for you without a reason, but that no one ever does anything bad to you unless there is a reason as long as sickness or mental illness is not a factor. Certainly, when a mother kills her babies or young children, that is a sign of a mental aberration; or when Jeffrey Dahmer killed many young men, raped them, and then stuffed them in his freezer, that too was indicative of mental imbalance. Such are not the type of individuals of which the proverb speaks. Although Timothy McVeigh took a lot of innocent lives, as a follower of David Koresh (religious fanatic who took names of biblically famous King David [Judah] and Cyrus [Persia]), his bombing of the Oklahoma City Federal Building was a tit-for-tat event of which the proverb speaks for he was avenging the killing and burning of Koresh's cohort on the farm in Waco, Texas, by the governmental.

FBI agency, months earlier: The injustices carried out by the Western nations against Iran over the years certainly do not fit into the framework of the proverb either for my injured homeland never provoked such behavior. The false propaganda, ill will, and malevolent wrongdoings are more in the category of mental aberration than revenge; and this type of international mayhem must be obliterated!

Certainly, the poor strategy of Russia and the West against Iran derived from the misapprehension that if Iran was to become too powerful, these competing nations would lose out on benefits from oil and other business ventures in the Middle East. Our appeal is to the intellectuals on both sides to lay aside the differences of the past and to try now to communicate and discuss the need for and the correctness in attempting to deal with each other in fair and equitable fashion.

Much better that both sides dispense with lies and demagoguery and end the punishment and killing of innocents in each other's backyards. All need to wake up and end these lunatic policies.

In other words, better to follow the teachings of Jesus Christ with regard to treating another as one himself would prefer to be treated. Peace on earth, love even of enemies, and respect for the downtrodden must become the byword of human relations. The deceptions of Abraham with Abimelek and the trickery of Jacob with Isaac must become matters of the past and be replaced by the integrity of Christianity! The aims of politicians must be concern for the other guy and compassion for humanity, no longer one for upmanship, discrimination, and deceit. When love prevails, all problems can be solved; and al Qaeda, Hezbollah, Hamas terrorism, and domestic violence of the McVeigh sort will be no more! If we really want to change the course of history, this is the new way that must prevail!

Point Three

3. Concerning the USA: Following the Second World War, England and Europe were countries that had to deal with severe physical damage to their cities and countryside whereas the United States had been left virtually untouched by war's devastation.

Much like a new imperial Rome, the United States appeared in the world's arena as victor. All of the former Allies readily admitted that without the assistance of the United States and its military forces, there indeed could have been no victory. England and Europe decided to cooperate in the effort to maintain friendly relations with the North American continent in order to continue to utilize the help that they still so badly needed, especially in the endeavors to rebuild their political, military, and petroleum dependencies. The Old World knew quite fundamentally that it could not accomplish goals formerly set for themselves in the Middle East without the close backing of the United States. This realization easily overcame the hesitancy that they felt deep down within their hearts that they regretted to approach on bended knee the former colony across the Atlantic that once had been a colonial dependency. The Middle East was a most difficult area to maintain control over without bringing the United States and its economic and technological capabilities to the task. Rather than outright competition with one another as in the past, with regard to the oil fields of the Middle East and elsewhere, they decided to cut the United States into the picture and derive the benefits of this new corporate alliance.

For example, the oil fields were shared as follows: Those of Saudi Arabia and Bahrain were designated for supplying the United States while those of Kuwait were to be split between England and the United States—40 percent for each, with a smaller percentage for France (whose chief supplier was Africa). In exchange for this seemingly generous sharing, the shrewdness of England and Europe was that they also shifted the main weight of global problems to the shoulders of their new North American colleagues, and major portions of the social and military expenses involved in addressing these international conundrums were now destined to fall to the political and financial responsibility of the United States. In essence, England and the European countries slipped the onus of major international complexities onto the plate of the United States in exchange for a share in the oil of the Middle East. One such situation was the relation of France to Vietnam, a losing proposition for the French that was eventually posited at the feet of the United States who assumed the role of military opponent in that Far Eastern nation under the guise of fighting to save that part of the world from the Communists. And in fact, most of the Cold War was laid on the back of the United States along with serious ethnic and religious conflicts involving Yugoslavia, Bosnia, Israel and its neighbors, and, eventually, Iraq.

Eventually, the important role of lobbyists for Israel in the United States would determine the direction of this new position of the United States in international intrigues. Better to understand this area of developing global relations with is material supplied in an excellent text published in March of 2006 and written by two professors of political science, Dr. John J. Mearsheimer of the University of Chicago and Dr. Stephen Walt of the faculty of the Kennedy School of Government at Harvard University. The book is entitled *The Israel Lobby and U.S. Foreign Policy*. The study is an unbiased and professionally sound analysis regarding this area of interest and is extremely helpful in approaching an understanding of this theme.

4. The extreme significance of the establishment of the nation of Israel is my final point of consideration. A very vigilant and studied approach by England—taking into account many matters including religion, economics, political and military psychology, and the likelihood of acceptance or nonacceptance—led to the establishment of the nation of Israel in their Palestinian location. Final considerations centered upon either Argentina or Palestine as the place to establish this colony. Following the very careful study

of the matter to which I have alluded, the English masterminds charged with this strategic decision chose Palestine as the proper site for establishment of this new homeland. The decision was ultimately founded upon a need to make sure that key resources of oil, money, and political mastery would always be positioned in an area of control easily accessible to England and its allies. The choice was an omphalos of great wisdom and cautious planning of maximum benefit to those involved. I would best characterize the thinking that resulted in the selection of Palestine as the Oil Plan for if the Middle East were devoid of that resource, then the settlement of Israel in Palestine could have been anywhere else of strategic importance due to the wide dispersion of the Jewish people.

And of course, the selection of Palestine was quite acceptable and beneficial to the Jewish Diaspora because of their long-held belief that the territory of what once was the land of the race of humanity chosen by God should ultimately be the seat of their governance—the Promised Land. But for the Arabs and Palestinians, it was not beneficial nor acceptable. The settlement meant the displacement of these poor peoples from territory that had been in their ownership for many years. Not a single country of the Arab world could approve this affront to their fellow Muslims. Iraq, Egypt, Syria, Jordan, Saudi Arabia—every last Arab nation—rejected the plan that seemed, quite obviously, to create conflict between two peoples of a common ethnic background but of distinctly divergent religious customs.

The matter that I again emphasize is that although the terms of settlement seemed, quite inequitably, to favor the people to be known as the Israelis, in fact, the whole strategy by design was to provide a real benefit to the colonizing English and company who, for the sake of access to oil, placed the Jewish colony smack-dab in the center of an established Arab domain (and not in Argentina). The question that is at the crux of this circumstance can only be, "Should a people dispersed throughout the world for nearly eighteen centuries and without a conventionally understood homeland for all these many years be forcibly imposed into the territory of a settled people and allowed to displace them from soil that had become their home and the very heart of their existence, meager as that existence might seem?"

Were the hearts of the English perpetrators of this plan truly burning for these dispersed peoples, and were they acting out of a compassion for the Diaspora that exceeded all bounds, comparable to or even exceeding an assumed motherhood? I believe that the informed answer to this question can only rightfully be no! An extreme concern (as a Persian concept puts it, "More Catholic even than the pope") cannot, on any truthful basis, be identified in this contrived international decision. The actual basis for the ultimate outcome was a selfish caring for personal ambitions rather than a pity for wandering peoples. The establishment of the new Jewish nation and government, with all its inequitable ramifications and resulting antipathies as we now have come to realize those hatreds, were carried out to satisfy a greed for oil rather than to nurture an abused child.

Not feeling fully assured that the international community would accept or approve of this presumptuous stratagem, both England and the United States gave only de facto recognition to the newly established State of Israel. Russia alone gave full recognition to the fledgling nation. In the hope of nipping a horrible incipience in the bud, Iraq, Egypt, and Jordan sent armies immediately to attack the infant colony; and without the military assistance of those governments that had contrived the Oil Plan, it would have been impossible for the new Israel to survive the assault of its Arab enemies. And as the realization of the benefits to be derived from this "buffering" establishment grew to maturity, the founding nation (England) and its allies (including the United States) granted de jure recognition to the "new kid on the block." Ambassadors were exchanged in 1951; and the issuance of a bond amounting to five hundred million dollars on that time, to the State of Israel, sealed the full establishment of that nation among the international community. Dr. Chaim Weizmann, a leader of the Zionist party and a famous chemist, was elected as first president of the newly constituted Jewish government. Continuing financial support from the United States, abetted by investments by its large Jewish population, ensured the successful footing of the new state as a pecuniary entity on the world scene.

Several asides at this point are appropriate. Note 1: The success of Israel militarily against its Arab foes benefitted England, Russia, and the United States. A number of wars between the Arab states and Israel provided success for the reinforced Jewish entity, and revenue from Middle East oil sales lined the pockets of the colonizers beyond their wildest imaginings, ensuring the continuance of the cat and mouse games throughout the ensuing years.

Although major portions of the "good people" of these Western and Russian nations were oblivious to the Oil Plan fomented by their governments, the reality of what was taking place is nonetheless established. The Iraq wars were also initiated deceptively. The influence of the Israeli lobby has not been an obvious factor in these developments, and no clear-cut set of inciting actions are apparent. Notwithstanding, a large segment of the so-called good people of these outside countries are saddened by events in the Middle East, and the question of whether oil has greater value than human existence is a growing inquiry among intellectuals and concerned citizens.

Note 2: The Security Council of the United Nations held a meeting on November 16, 2006, in which they condemned the killing by Israel of nineteen Palestinians in Beit Hanoun. This action against Israel was approved by all countries including Europe but was vetoed by the United States.

Note 3: The famous English publication the *Guardian* carried an article in November 2006 in which the statement appeared that many people wish that the "new imperial Rome" (USA) would someday be overthrown. (I suggest that, in part, this wish is already fulfilled since President George W. Bush is now diminished in the history of the United States.) The author of the article declared that the dignity and trustworthiness of the United States had been destroyed throughout the world and most certainly in the Middle East. It was further asserted that the European Parliament severely condemned the treatment of prisoners at Guantanamo and Abu Ghraib and that the violation of human rights in these detention centers was deplorable. The conclusion was that the United States deserved such condemnation and that it must be held accountable just as any other country would for such flagrant disregard for human dignity. "Justice for all" as stated in the Pledge of Allegiance of the United States applies to all nationalities as well as to its own citizens.

Note 4: A brief overview of the history of Palestine might be in order at this juncture. We recall that after 1000 BC, imperial Egypt had weakened considerably. The Hebrew people took advantage of this opportunity in order to establish a government in Palestine for the first time. The combined forces of Saul and David overcame numerous sources of opposition in Palestine, and Solomon expanded the Jewish kingdom all the way to the Gulf of Aqaba. The Hebrew government was then divided into Israel and Judah. Judah was under the House of David while Israel was eventually engulfed by Assyria in 722 BC and after dispersion and intermingling with their conquerors was a region more familiarly known as Samaria. Then by 586 BC, Judah was invaded and overpowered by Babylonia, which kingdom had defeated Assyria and which, in turn, fell, to the upsurge of the kingdom of Persia, which assumed much of the control of the inhabited area of what is today known as the Middle East as well as much of southern Europe. The Persians granted much more autonomy to conquered territories; and eventually, a new Jewish state was reestablished with Jerusalem at its center and with Zerubbabel, Nehemiah, and Ezra as governmental and religious leaders.

In the fourth century BC, Alexander the Great occupied Palestine, which was then a somewhat disorganized grouping of Jewish and Bedouin settlements. There always existed a yearning to reunite into a Hebrew state, and finally in 141 BC, the Hebrew family Maccabee was able to initiate a cohesion of forces sufficient to create briefly for seventy years the facsimile of a Jewish state within the area of Palestine with Jerusalem as its center; but finally in 71 BC, this whole territory became subject to the Roman Empire, and the vestiges of a new Israel disappeared until modern times. When Jesus Christ was born, the Palestinian territory was under the rule of one of the Herods; but he, in turn, was subject to the governance of the Roman Empire. Several attempts to rise up against Roman rule were made—such as in AD 66 when a revolt ended with the destruction by Rome of the Jewish temple in Jerusalem in AD 70 and with the forceful dispersion of many of the Jews from that area and that of the lesser bloody insurrection of AD 132 that ended any pretension of the diminished Hebrew colony surviving as a unified entity. Most fled to Europe and Russia.

In AD 640, Palestine came under Islamic control and the rule of Omar, the second in succession to Mohammed. Muslim domination of this territory continued through the ninth century when the Fatimite dynasty (one kind of Shiite government)— which claimed descent from Fatimah, daughter of Mohammed, and which once ruled in Egypt—assumed control of Palestine and destroyed all non-Muslim places of worship, devastating the encampments of pilgrims protesting other than the Islamic faith. The Fatimites were eventually overthrown and replaced by followers of Saladin, the greatest of Muslim warriors who, in turn, was challenged by crusaders and who eventually, through truce with the Europeans, allowed the establishment of some Christian colonies in coastal Palestine and even in Jerusalem. At about the start of the twelfth century, peoples of Turkish origin known as Mamelukes began to exert their influence throughout Asia Minor and actually controlled the region of Palestine for nearly 250 years until they were challenged by Utman, a Turkish caliph, and displaced from their position of dominance by the Ottoman Turks who exercised authority over Palestine from about 1516 on until the end of World War I. Even after the Mamelukes were defeated in Palestine, they maintained control in Egypt until about 1800 when Napoleon I finally ended their rule there.

During all this time, there were continual struggles between Muslims and Christians in Palestine. Colonies of Jews continued in the eighteenth century in dispersion throughout Europe and Russia. Efforts of groups of Jews to return to Palestine began to materialize, and in 1870, the first such cohort known as Pitah Tiqua was formed and migrated back to Palestine. From 1882 to 1914, increasing numbers of the Jewish Diaspora in Russia made their way back to the Jewish homeland. The first Zionist political party organized in Palestine in 1877; and in 1917 and 1918, that territory emerged from Turkish control and, as a spoil of the First World War, became a colony of Great Britain.

During and immediately after the Second World War, greater numbers of Jewish immigrants began arriving in Palestine—a situation which was opposed by England at first. Despite this opposition, however, the unlawful immigration continued unabated. Following the end of the war, a joint body known as the Commission of the United States and England for the Jewish Problem was established to manage the circumstances; and eventually, the setting up of the new State of Israel in Palestine became reality. As previously emphasized, the Arab people have never accepted this state of affairs, and conflict in the Middle East is ongoing. And may I also reiterate that the parties responsible for the conditions that have led up to this interminable conflict are the Western countries that chose Palestine as the site for the Jewish homeland. When we read or hear of a Palestinian suicide bomber blowing up a Jewish bus or of bombs being dropped on a Palestinian enclave with the ensuing loss of innocent lives, let us be cautious about the vehemence with which we castigate the Arabs or Jews for the conditions that allow these dastardly deeds were framed by none other than our own governments of the United States and of England. So often, the majority of the good people of the West are totally unaware of what has been done—not for the benefit of any of the innocent victims of this most unfortunate conflict, but rather for the sake of access to and use of oil for the nations represented by our former Western diplomats.

And recall also the ironic fact that the origins of al Qaeda and the Taliban in Afghanistan were their empowerment by the West to withstand the invading Russians in order to prevent the USSR from reaching the Persian Gulf and its huge reserves of oil—the largest in the world! When we reflect upon the tragedy of 9/11, let us at least realize the part that we played in the materializing of the terrorist groups that fomented these horrible misdeeds. Humility should be a shared virtue. The importance of Iran from the point of view of its resources of oil and natural gas and from the standpoint of its strategic position is unparalleled. And it is because of this circumstance, as I have previously indicated, that Western powers imposed this fanatic group of Islamic mullahs upon a people to keep them in an inferior position and cut off from the rest of the world. These theocrats have destroyed Iran: over one million intellectuals were murdered; and nearly three million of the cream of intelligentsia were forced to flee their homes, their work, and their fortunes in a humiliating exile. A senseless war with Iraq resulted in the deaths of over another million young people with no justification whatsoever. The Islamic overlords created Hezbollah and many other terrorist factions. The country of Iran was altered from a nation with a proud historic heritage to a country of disrepute. This situation was the intangible political strategy that resulted in the denial of the hapless people of Iran of any opportunity for real progress.

There is little connection between the people of Iran and the conflict between Israel and Palestine considering there is no accidental interest and common border between Iran and Israel, but because of the Islamic tyrants ruling Iran at this time, billions of dollars are presently being spent for the benefit of the Hamas faction in Palestine and for other terrorist groups. This is in spite of the fact that many Iranian people are suffering in poverty without jobs or money. The Western media and politicians are holding all of Iran responsible for these actions, yet it is really only the imposed regime that is carrying out this unilateral action in opposition to the West and especially versus the United

States—ironically, the very powers that surreptitiously installed the kleptocratic regime in the first place.

Note 5 (the role of Iraq): a factor of major significance and, in reality, mainly because of their huge resource of oil. The country was invaded by the United States and Britain on the pretexts of Saddam Hussein developing weapons of mass destruction and also having been involved in the fomenting of the horrendous attack on the United States on 9/11. A real concern by the governing powers of these Western allies was that Saddam's authority posed a real threat to the future security of Israel. Saddam was overthrown, but in the process, many thousands of innocent Iraqis have been killed either by the invaders or later by the insurgents. Ironically, the course of events has led to the death of more U.S. soldiers than hapless victims killed on 9/11; and many more U.S. servicemen have suffered the loss of eyes, limbs, and psychological balance. The justification for these consequences is not easy to reason, but the situation is interpreted as appropriate "for the sake of freedom." Indeed, a very costly freedom! In fact, a situation that should more properly be labeled as a misuse or abuse of freedom.

The covert strategies of the West causing loss of freedom for both Iranians and Afghans back in the seventies "for the sake of human rights" gave rise to the terrorist groups of al Qaeda, Hezbollah, and Hamas and to the further growth and development of established insurgents like the Taliban. Consider that if the misdirection of pressure from the West—climaxed peacefully in 1979—eventually led to the bitter world situation today, what will be the outcome of an even greater misapplication of military might today in Iraq "for the sake of freedom," and how will it affect the destiny of tomorrow's generations?

Chapter Four

The Dependency of Man

As we suggested in the preceding discussion, human life cannot exist without interdependency, not without insight and understanding of those who share this planet with us. Relationships with others result in success and happiness or in failure and sadness. Often, it is difficult to fathom the root cause for one's particular situation. For those who have a faith in God, there seems always to be hope beyond one's actual circumstance, and comfort is derived by considering one's condition to be concordant with the will of God.

Also, as previously discussed, there are several approaches to God. In the scientific approach, God is absolutely without need and is infinite. How do we arrive at an understanding of God from the viewpoint of a scientist? Scientists believe that if we know ourselves, then we are approaching an understanding of God and of the universe. Basically, it is the scientific approach that understanding and knowledge define the pathway that leads to God.

As previously suggested, human beings need to explore and thereby know as many avenues of knowledge as there are numbers of cells in the human body, probably some seventy trillion in estimated count.* By completely knowing each cell of our makeup, we are approaching a full understanding of our selves and of the universe and, hence, approaching a full awareness of God. To date, we have many successes in various fields of endeavor, such as geology, oceanography, space technology, medicine, and communication. But even with the advances that we enjoy in these various categories, the knowledge count that this might be estimated at would only possibly be eight or nine billion or about the population of today's planet earth. To reach a knowledge potential of seventy trillion, one thus realizes that we have a long way to go toward infinite understanding, or knowledge of every cell in the human body. At such time as we have full knowledge of ourselves, of every one of the seventy trillion cells that compose our being, we would then have infinite understanding of ourselves and would be in a position of having attained life.* In a recent article in *Time* magazine (January 29, 2007) entitled "The Brain: A User's Guide," one of the contributing writers, Dr. Steven Pinker, Johnson professor of psychology at Harvard, points out that the total cell count in the brain is about one trillion cells.

How can we possibly overcome this gap in our understanding, from eight or nine billion to seventy trillion? The answer to that challenge lies in the human passion for exploration, knowledge, and power. It is this fertile potential that will supply the energy to fill in this huge hiatus.

Scientists believe that there are millions of billions of stars and planets that have not yet been discovered—let alone having been named. And in our oceans and deserts, there remain myriads of plants and creatures yet to be catalogued and provided appropriate nomenclature. And out in the universe, there remain planets with the proper conditions to support life, possibly with essentials and details other than those of our own planet earth who are seeking to reach out to us, even as we are attempting to communicate with them.

The diaphanous quality of mysteries beyond our own creation provide a lure that will invite the probing, exploratory mind of man for years to come and will eventually assist in the narrowing of the unknown and the ineluctable fortunate happenstance of the discovery of God, the intelligent power that created the universe with a sophisticated agenda and system beyond human intelligence and fathoming. Such a magnificent comprehension will most certainly be delayed because of our human limitations and the unlimitedness of God. The unlimited character of this creator really has no dependency, such as a need to be worshiped, nor a reliance upon angels for assistance nor the adversarial challenge of its power by a Satan. However, a sense of loneliness may be inferred from the Genesis account of the Bible on this matter when God expresses the wish to create man in his image (Genesis 1:26).

Calculations by scientists have proposed an age for the universe and for some stars and planets. By such calculations, there is proof suggesting that certain other heavenly bodies—such as the earth, the sun, and the moon—did not exist; let us say some star existed fourteen billion years ago. So since that time, a coming into being of these additional entities has occurred—sun, ten billion years; earth, four or five billion years. The U.S. space program is working out details, and a cause and effect are implied. So we assume a creator—God in English, Khoda in Farsi—of all humans and of the sun, the moon, and the earth. Further, this creator is limitless, is without needs, and is absolute love.

Each individual may have a different interpretation and a different relationship with their god. If we imagine that each one of the eight or nine billion in the population of the world today may have a distinct variation in their perception of God, what should we do? The visual intellectuals have a solution. They argue that each individual has the right to believe what he or she imagines to be right—that is, where there is freedom of religion and of thought. However, in this twenty-first century, some ideological regimes, like Communism and Islam, deprive their subjects of such independence.

For example, Rumi has a story in his famous book *Masnavi* about a shepherd who, one day while watching his sheep and quietly praying for his needs, suddenly conceived a vision of God in the form of a beautiful girl. He began cooing and murmuring, "Where are you, my god?" and he had pleasant thoughts of touching the girl's hair and face and washing her body with tender caresses.

As he was meditating in this enraptured fashion, he heard Moses speak in a harsh and stern voice, "Shut up! This is blasphemy!" The shepherd was startled and sad, and he cried out loud in a very upset manner.

Meantime, God responded to Moses by asking him why he had upset his servant. "Everyone has a right to speak to me with his own understanding in any way that he imagines me and with any fancy that befalls him. You have spoken harshly to him in his reverie and have distressed him and have caused him to become separated from me rather than to maintain the close connection to me that had been established. I sent you to assist people in making connection with me rather than to cause a division between us. If a person has accomplished a close relationship with me, such a relationship is not to be disturbed or broken. They may pray or meditate with whatever fantasy they have achieved. There is no special place, no special words, nor any special garment or requirement for such meditation to occur!" Mevlevi was one of the dervishes founded by Jalal ad-Din Muhammad Rumi, a famous mystic poet and a most learned man in the year AD 1273

Another interesting approach to this idea occurred to me when I was in Najaf, Iraq, in 1954, studying to become a mullah. It was during one of my classes at the center for religious study, during a session, occurring each day between 2 and 4 p.m. and devoted to an interpretation of the Koran. The professor leading the class was named Assad Allah (lion of Allah), and he was very strict. Before the Koran was opened in a period of study, he required each of us ten students to perform ablution. Ritual ablution consists of washing the hands, the mouth, the face, the arms, and the first three toes as well as touching the forehead from the center to the side, all in a very sequential and exact manner. If a student protested that he had already performed ablution that day, the professor insisted that that did not matter for each of us may have passed flatus that day without realizing it—an event that would most certainly have rendered us "unclean." The words of the Koran (Arabic: "La Yamasahu Ela Mot a Heroon") state that "No one can touch the Koran unless they are clean." This is interpreted in varying manner, and ablution is one alternative. There follows this extended digression.

Well, one day, when we were studying the Baqarah, which is one of the largest sura (chapter or section) of the Koran and which discusses how God creates humans as his successors and how Satan came into being, the professor described how Allah announced to all the angels that he was going to create man who would be different from an angel in that man would have freedom to choose whether or not to obey God. The angels asked why for they feared that—since they were present to worship and obey God—if he created human beings with freedom, they might just not follow God's commands and might cause corruption and crime. God responded by saying, "I know all things, and you are not able to know what I know." Furthermore, he told the angels that they were to bow down to the humans, which all were willing to do except for one angel named Satan. As God created man from dust, he blew his spirit into this new creation, exclaiming that "This is my *best* creation!" Satan, because of his pride, pointed out to God that as an angel, he had been brought forth from fire; and since fire is superior to dust, he could not possibly bow down to one created from an inferior source. Satan was angered, our professor indicated, at first because as an angel, he had served the master for six thousand years in obedience, a length of time that seemed inviolable.

After this expression of rebellion, God cursed Satan; but instead of destroying him, he decided to expel him or cast him out of his kingdom, declaring that he would allow him to remain in existence as long as he himself did. And Satan replied, "Now I will cause your human creatures to disobey you!" And so, the eternal struggle of good and evil was initiated.

Professor Assad Allah further explained three things, viz, angel, human, and jinn and the thing as follows: Angels are unable to sin or disobey God. They may assume a variety of faces, such as that of a human, a cat, or even a cow. But they may not have the face of a dog or a pig.

Humans, as I have emphasized, enjoy freedom, even to sin or to disobey God. They are able to do good or bad as they choose, but they do not appear with the face of an animal, such as a cat or a cow. Humans are the successors of God on earth as previously mentioned.

Jinn can appear with any kind of face—human, cat, cow, dog, or pig. Jinn have the same duties and responsibilities to God as do human beings, but they do have the freedom to obey or to sin.

It was at this point in his discourse that one of the professor's students and my classmate by the name of Sheik Mansour Rafei, a blue-eyed lad with brown hair who was from a mountain village in Northern Iran, raised a question about Satan. "As you have explained it, Satan was an angel. Since all angels were not able to disobey God, how could this angel become like a human being and defy an order from God? And furthermore," Sheik Mansour continued, "how could an ordinary human being become the successor of God on earth? Could God die and require a mortal to replace him? And as Shiites claim, could a human and mortal being such as Mohammed be God's successor yet later himself die and be replaced by Abū Bakr . . . or Imam Ali . . . as a successor as Shiites further believe?"

Sheik Mansour also further queried the professor concerning the existence of jinns. "We cannot find any creature in existence here on earth having the name and role of jinn. They are supposed to be similar to humans, with the same responsibilities. They must accept Islam and worship God, but where are they? We can't see them and never encounter them, yet every section of the Koran that explains the duties of humans to God also mentions the duties of jinns to God. Furthermore, the professor said the Koran states, 'Ma-khalakto-al-jinn-o-val-ens-o-ella-le-yabodune.'" " in English " We create humans and jinns to know and to worship God." Sheik Mansour then concluded, "In what part of the world do the jinns dwell?"

Dismayed, the professor responded to the impertinence of the young Iranian by saying, "Don't you realize that if someone poses enigmatic questions, such as those you have raised, and challenges the authority of that sacred text, such as you have done, that person will have their rear end seared by fire?"

At this juncture, whether by chance or by spite, the student passed flatus in an audible manner; his face flushed, and he left the room, blurting out, "You forced everyone including me to do ablution before entering this class. Maybe," he continued, "I might have committed another sin unknown to you that would have obligated me to undergo complete immersion, *ghusl*, before entering this class today!"

The professor became furious and screamed, "You are like Satan, scheming and malicious! You are cursed and do not deserve to become a soldier of twelfth Imam!"** All students at this Shiite

---

*   Ghusl is the Islamic religious meaning for the form of ablution that is the complete immersion of the body by plunging into water and thoroughly washing after the ejaculation of semen, either by masturbation or intercourse.

** Twelfth Imam: Shiite Muslims believe that the twelfth Imam was a religious leader who never died and is one who watches over human beings and will someday return and remove all injustice, oppression, and sorrow from his followers as well as bring them peace, understanding, and everlasting righteousness. Those who are unbelievers will be slain by his powerful sword.

Muslim school were considered to be in this category of the faithful, and to be degraded in this manner in front of the other classmates was a matter of extreme shame and embarrassment. The fellow students who were present laughed at him in derision. Further, the professor announced that because of his impertinence, he would not be allowed to remain at school and would be expelled. At this, some of the fellow clansmen began to beg for forgiveness for the hapless lad, but the professor became more adamant and declared,

"Be quiet! I have no personal bias, and everything that I am saying and doing is for the sake and honor of God and of his holy book, the Koran!" The student, Mansour, returned to his room and locked himself in, refusing any visitors—not even close friends—for a week. Then silently, he disappeared and, as it was later learned, went back to Iran but not to his northern mountain village, rather to Tehran. It also was learned that he exchanged the clothes of a student mullah (sleeveless tunic) for those of a young Western-style adherent. He totally rejected his Muslim traditions and, quite naturally, was afraid to reveal his altered lifestyle to anyone, not even his immediate family. He experienced a very difficult period financially but was eventually able to gain employment in Tehran as a bus driver's assistant, taking tickets from passengers as they boarded the bus.

Eventually, on a cold rainy night, the bus stopped at the terminal; and one of his former mullah classmates entered the bus and gave his fare to the bus driver's assistant, Mansour, who recognized his former fellow student and returned his fare, saying, "You, my colleague, be my guest!"

The traveler, not recognizing Mansour, replied, "Thank you a lot, and may God bless you!"

In a jocose vein, Mansour retorted, "You are very welcome, but did you undergo ablution before you entered this vehicle?"

The astounded passenger, still not recognizing Mansour, exclaimed, "Such, sir, is none of your business!" Befuddled, the mullah further muttered, "Fools have the best luck!"

To which the anxious driver's assistant replied, "Do you know Professor Sayad Assad Allah?"

The amazed passenger stared closely at the driver assistant's shaved face and crop of oily brown hair and shortly, after recognition, shouted the name, "Mansour!" They then exchanged friendly greeting, but situational circumstances denied them further exchange of conversation at that time, and the overwhelmed traveler reached his destination at the next station and departed the bus.

After two months, the mullah returned to school at Najaf and shared his experience with other students who had been close friends and classmates of the departed rebel. He described how he had encountered Mansour, adding that he had become an absolute kafir, or a "hapless infidel."

Not only had Mansour changed his attire, but he had also changed his name to Hushang Shahreyari.

He worked his bus job mostly by day but spent his evenings at a school where he studied natural science and biology. After three years of afterwork study in this field, he achieved a degree in it and was able to enter medical school. During this period of transition, he met Dr. Mojtahedi, the director of Alborz Educational Foundation and the founder of the Industrial University of Aryamehr. Dr. Mojtahedi has devoted his life to assisting students in financial need, and he was extremely helpful to Mansour. There was a competition for overseas medical study, and he advised Mansour to apply for that opportunity, which he did and won an all-expenses-paid scholarship for medical study in Paris as well as a prize of two thousand dollars, without requirement for repayment, to meet personal needs during the time of that preparation—this prize was awarded by Pahlavi's charity foundation.

While he was in Paris, a longtime friend of his from his hometown in Northern Iran was living in Frankfurt, Germany. This friend was married to a German lady and had three children. The family invited Mansour to visit them for a week during winter break. "You bring your wine from Paris, and we will enjoy our German beer together!" Mansour accepted the invitation, and while he was there, they went to church together on Sunday. The wife and children enjoyed the Christian fellowship, and on that particular Sunday, there was a special program. Mansour indicated that there would be no problem in his joining them for the occasion since he was a kafir and was considered by his Islamic associates to be a hopeless infidel and an outcast of the Muslim faith. After two hours of an enjoyable worship experience, his friend asked Mansour what his opinion of the particular service had been inasmuch as he had been a student at Najaf studying to be a leader in the Shiite sect of the Mohammedan religion.

He replied that he was no longer a follower of Islam since his ignominious departure from the training center at Najaf and that he was particularly interested in the fact that the god that his good friend and family worshiped could receive adulation in French, German, and Arabic, and at any time whereas the god of Muslims seemed only to accept praise and adoration in Arabic and only at specific times—such as before sunrise, at noon, in the afternoon before sunset, at sunset, and again before midnight. "And each time," he stated further, "those who pray to the god Allah must turn themselves toward Mecca while you pray facing in any and all directions!"

He further emphasized that in the past, he had difficulty with these restrictions but that "in this service of worship, there seemed not only to be freedom in the language spoken and the stance assumed, but also a spirit of love and mutual concern." He also recited an Iranian poem that he had committed to memory that described the worship of God as an opportunity for people to express a concern to help and to serve people of all backgrounds worldwide! Such spontaneous outpouring of gratitude is not limited to certain chants and specific phrases or type of dress but rather represents an offering of love for that god and that god's creation. In return, that god demands only trust in goodness and mercy and forgiveness—a powerful expression of thanksgiving and love!

Mansour climaxed this conversation by saying, "I was moved by this service. It provided the sort of help that I am seeking . .

. relief from disturbing thoughts from the past. I plan to pursue this new interest that has been provided. Thank you!"

His friend replied, "We knew this and hoped that during this visit, we might be able to elevate your spirit. It was my wife's idea to invite you to our home and church for a time, hoping that this experience would boost your morale and comfort you spiritually."

The wife then inquired if Mansour had any especially foremost recollections of his religious studies at Najaf, Iraq. He answered that he had a few, particularly when the professor beat him on the head with his walking stick because he asked questions about his lecture. He then added some details, "The professor's name was Fazel Kayeni and was very tall, about six feet five. He had been a famous wrestler in the village of Kayen. At the time, he was teaching about the prophet Meraj, a Shiite who taught that Allah flew the prophet Mohammed from his mosque in the Medina to Jerusalem on a horse named Doldol and also carried Mohammed with him to the first heaven where he saw Adam. Following this, he transported Mohammed to subsequent heavens where he saw other prophets, including Jesus in seventh heaven. Mohammed asked each prophet that he met a different question, and he always received an answer."

Mansour continued, "While the professor was describing this, I asked how come Mohammed could fly to the different heavens and finally land in Jerusalem? The professor replied, 'According to the Koran, Allah wanted to show his reflection to Mohammed. The Koran says, "Sobhanah-al-lazi, A-sra be-abdehi-lailan, men-al mas ged-al heram."' The professor continued, 'Recall, I went to the Baghdad airport and flew to the Tehran airport in less than an hour. I was able to do that on an airplane built by humans. Surely, Allah has the ability to take his prophet Mohammed from the earth to the seven heavens in order to demonstrate his power.' With that utterance, he struck me on the back of my head with his walking stick. Although my head did not bleed, for a long time, I had pain there. The professor then added, 'Mansour, don't talk like indecent Europeans do.' I asked, 'What do those Europeans believe?' He replied, 'The Koran states that Mohammed broke the moon in two. But the Europeans declare that if he had done that, it surely would have been recorded in history and that since it is not historic, it could not have happened.' Then the professor quoted the Koran, 'Alef-laam-mim-ekta-raba-to-al-saat-van-shakah-al-kamar.'"

Finally, the wife of Mansour's friend said, "I never heard of such outlandish things, and I am sorry that you had such bad experiences at Najaf. We certainly should respect all others' beliefs, even if we feel that they are mere superstition."

It is my considered view that the problem in Islam is that Muslims are intolerant of anyone who questions a statement of the Koran or who expresses an idea contrary to their belief. Certainly, the story of what happened to Mansour is an unquestionable illustration of my opinion and would explain why so many like him would find the Christian faith to be like grace sent from heaven!

Chapter Five

Religious Roots and Political Principles

Let us now initiate our consideration of the entity of religion; after all, it is our stated purpose for this writing to provide a comparative commentary on some of the major religions of our human race. Let us also state forthrightly that we honor and respect all religious expression and that in no way will we pass judgment upon the validity of the content of any of the formal world religions nor upon the sincerity of their adherents. We certainly are in no position to do such a thing. Our intention is to provide unbiased information insofar as it is possible and, where feasible, to contrast rudiments of a particular faith with the foundations of another.

In general, the roots of a religion derive largely from tribal concerns and/or philosophical attitudes. For example, the Jewish religion was initiated in the tribe of Abraham whereas the Islamic faith originated in the tribal traditions of Koreish, an offshoot of Abraham. On the other hand, the Hindu, Buddhist, Jain, Vedic, and Confucian religions all have largely contemplative origins. The Christian religion builds upon Jesus Christ, but it has a series of historical events marking its initiation, the key to which is the birth of Jesus to the Virgin Mary and the Holy Spirit, that does not belong to any tribe or philosophical attitudes.

Because of the current focus of events upon the Middle East and the war in Iraq as well as the struggle of al Qaeda (terrorism) with the West, largely in the confines of the Muslim world, our initial concerns will be with the three major religions of that region—namely, Judaism, Christianity, and Islam. Our endeavor will be to better understand the historic foundations of these three faiths as well as possibly to discover grounds for understanding among them so as to offer solutions to seeming dilemmas that contribute to the perpetuation of strife among them. At all times, it would seem that interfaith communication might more effectively arrive at understanding, even if deficient, and allow for some rapprochement in place of bitterness, contention, and hostility—ending only in recrimination and outright war such as we are currently experiencing.

Presently, Western countries are battling in behalf of freedom while those of Eastern persuasion struggle in the name of God. The stated allegiances are most certainly universally revered; doctrines supported by freedom and by God are certainly valued on all sides. Is it really possible that these two idealized values would really be struggling against each other? Might freedom and God actually be opposing forces? Would God wage war against freedom, and vice versa? Are the two principles feasibly contradictory?

As previously stated, "God is without need at all." He does not require man to kill others in order to gain access to heaven. Revengeful colonization, domineering force, and terrorization are the results of man's needs than they are of possessive requirements of God. Because of his limitless power beyond nature and his omnipresence beyond the endless universe, there can be no imagined need that God has that would require elimination of another (even though adherents of al Qaeda believe such action is necessary).

At the creation of mankind, God invested individuals with freedom of thought, allowing them to grow in their self-understanding and in knowledge of the universe. Without such freedom of thought, it is impossible to increase in understanding nor to secure physical and spiritual needs. The reasoning process that al Qaeda, Hezbollah, and other Muslim extremists adopt to excuse their killing and bombing "for the sake of God" is certainly unacceptable; but it must also be recalled that for years, the Western powers colonized Middle Eastern countries and plundered their oil and wealth and that in 1948, the State of Israel was established without consulting or seeking comment from any Arab state, much less the state of Palestine, concerning the propriety of such an establishment. Israel then must logically be considered as having usurped their presence in this territory and to have assumed rights that were never other than "man-made" by an enemy force imposed from without. In what way, therefore, can the West assume that its motives and methods represent the ideal of freedom? In addition, Israel continues to destroy the lives of many innocent Palestinian children, women, and men as a security precaution—a security that the USA, in particular, and other Western nations peculiarly and blatantly support.

Furthermore, Middle Eastern Arab countries have not had the military resources or modern technology with which to defend themselves against Israel. Their Muslim faith derived from the very land that was taken from them, and the loss of land bequeathed upon them the right to revenge each life lost, thus justifying them in their belief that Allah approved of their taking of the lives of their enemies by bombing and mayhem as a fitting retribution. Such is their interpretation of "justification."

On the other hand, Western nations have two different policies in their relations with others—a domestic and a foreign policy. When it comes to domestic policy, individuals involved with that process enjoy individual rights such as are usually identified with true democracy and as are identified with the constitutional Bill of Rights. I personally have experienced all of these rights after I became a citizen of the United States but not while I was still a dweller in the Middle East, a phenomenon understood by other intellects of Arab countries.

Unfortunately, Western foreign policy is grounded in the Sophist Protagoras philosophy, which is immersed in falsehood and deception, without decent moral standard. Selfishness and benefits for the perpetrator are supreme, and subjects suffer. When the West employs military force in dealing with other countries "in the name of freedom," the result is quite the opposite of what occurs in the domestic situation, and demeaning and colonizing effects are the experience of those with whom they deal. Freedom is hardly the feeling promoted, and the actions of the oppressor seem more to symbolize a greed for the resources of the oppressed and an urge to treat subjects more for strategic purposes than for democratic principles.

How much better to define freedom as it is understood in domestic policy rather than as it is conceived in the foreign protocol. And as a final digression, let me state simply that both Arabic countries who battle against Israel and those Western countries who provide Israel with support are guilty of lying and deception for both parties are untruthful in their effort to assert their point. And such untruth does not offer any solution to the problems that exist, but only confound the situation and create new difficulties.

For example, the year 1979 is remembered in terms of the justification of human rights. The Western powers exchanged Iran's ruling regime for an Islamic hagiocracy that absolutely destroyed the human rights of its citizens. More than three million Iranians were forced to flee their country, and over a million others were killed. In conjunction with those tragedies, Hezbollah and al Qaeda (or the Ghodse Corps) were established— evil entities with whom we are currently engaged in a war that cost us over a trillion dollars and three thousand lives in 9/11 alone. Add to that mayhem the ongoing war in Iraq—which, in the name of freedom, has led to the flight from that country of over two million Iraqis, the death of millions more, and the expenditure of over seven hundred billion dollars by the USA, not to mention the nearly more than 3,500 sacred lives sacrificed by its embedded forces. It is mentioned in the book *Shah of Iran* that when Alexander the Great occupied the palace at Persepolis of Cyrus in Shiraz, he noted an inscription on a monument that was engraved with the following epigram: "My God, Ahura Mazda, keep my country from three calamities: drought, famine, and the lie." The importance of truth is further emphasized in the holy book of the Zoroastrians (Avesta): "Praise to the spirit of men who follow the truth, no matter in whatever place they were born. And praise to the spirit of women who follow the truth, no matter wherever they were born. And praise to both men and women who have or are or will strive to achieve victory for truth." As is implied, whenever there is a lie, problems ensue! Unfortunately, today's politics are synonymous with deception and falsehood. Too often in the political arena, whether foreign or domestic, any individual who is capable of deception will seem to be the one who is the more skillful, even though such success is short-lived and greater problems eventually are the issue.

Ss. Columba and Columban (AD 600) came to England and later to other countries in the continent of Europe to convert them to Christianity, and the people eventually did accept Christianity. Based upon this conversion, the peoples of these Western nations adopted a kind and considerate attitude toward their neighbors and strangers among them. But the foreign political policies of these countries have always reflected the influence of the Sophist Protagoras who argued that even a wrong idea can be used to argue and convince others that it is right; of Plato who was proponent of the idea that might makes right; and of Thrasymachus, the skeptic, who contended that there is no real good or evil and that the only proper concern is concern for oneself alone. These have been maintained as the basis for the foreign policies of Western society whereas domestic policy has embodied Christian love and concern for its nationals, foreign policy has reflected the cold ideology of the Greeks toward foreign peoples. In the West, there has been a distinct dichotomy in this way between domestic and foreign political policies, and national and international protocol clearly reflect these different reference points. The international attitudes of the United States are further influenced by one other force: the power of Israel's lobbyists in its political affairs and in the media (that is why both Republican and Democratic parties remain helpless before this unique pressure). To better understand this specific effect, an extensive and unbiased analysis of the Jewish and Islamic religions is required, and that is what is planned.

But first, a brief restatement of that with which we are confronted. Here in the West, we have two different—in fact, opposite or contrary—philosophies with which we are dealing. The majority regard their fellow citizens with an attitude of love and kindness and share a sense of equality. An ethical base undergirds domestic relationships. But in the area of foreign relationships, such an ethical base has been lacking. Self-interest is the predominant principle; and an inherent theme is the tacit approval of colonization, manipulation, and outright plunder, let us say, of third world countries. There has been an innate willingness to keep foreigners from improving and to take advantage of their ignorance and weaknesses. Such a slanted global policy has long underlaid the diplomacy of Western powers, but it is now beginning to be revealed for its shortcomings and is failing to find acceptance as a proper way to approach business or politics with Eastern colleagues. Such tyranny, deception, and dishonesty can no longer be employed without loss of trust. Adherence to truth and justice are proving to call forth the best and most effective results, especially between West and East.

Of course, such a superiority of moral probity has also been demonstrated in the relationships of all countries, even in situations of active opposition (combat) to one another. Three examples may be effectively provided.

The real reason for Napoleon's defeat at Waterloo was the moral determination of the English as contrasted to the lack of moral fiber and the more lackadaisical attitudes of the French, who could not overcome the energetic courage of the English. Now it is true that heavy rains and flooding had caused the heavy armament of the French to have become virtually unusable and that one of the French generals had become lost during his effort to try to prevent a German named Bleeker to join his forces with the English, but these disadvantages were not the main tactical causes for Napoleon's defeat. And while he made excellent use of these handicaps that Napoleon suffered at that battle, it was his conviction of the righteousness of his cause that drove the duke of Wellington and his men to extremes of bravery that really won the day for them. As strong as military might may be, it cannot outweigh or overcome the effectiveness of moral rectitude.

As example two, similar circumstances prevailed in World War II. Although the industrial and military strength of Hitler's juggernaut was initially superior, it was the moral conviction of the English, brought to focus by Winston Churchill, that eventually turned the tide. It was this determined resistance to Hitler's sluggish onslaught in the hectic early days of the 1940s that allowed time and events to evolve to the point that Russia and the USA were drawn into the conflict with their respective massive manpower and technology that ultimately led to the downfall of the German Wehrmacht. The solidification of the Allies was an incontrovertible force that brought down the ruthless Nazi leader, difficult as that struggle obviously was and varied as the ultimate ends of these Allies may have been.

The third example of the power of moral determination in the working out of historic events is more involved and abstruse. When Nāder Shāh, the Iranian emperor, attacked Muhammad Shah, the king of India, it was said that the reason for the defeat of the Indian king and the victory of the Iranian emperor were the torches carried by the Iranian soldiers on camels into the fray. It was believed that the flames of the torches frightened the elephants upon which the Indians rode and that their dismay led to the disruption and defeat of the Indian forces. This in part was true, but the king of India was wise and understood the culture of Iran, so there was a strategy involved. The Indian leader knew that if he surrendered, he would be protected and his fellow countrymen might be saved, even though some of the other Indian chiefs were at odds with this intuitive maneuver. Muhammad Shah approached Nāder Shāh, the Iranian emperor, and offered him his crown, placing it on his head and saying, "You are now the king of India." As Muhammad had suspected, Nāder Shāh kindly replaced the crown back upon Muhammad's head and declared that he should remain the king of India. In return, Muhammad Shah gave Nāder Shāh three priceless gifts in return: the great diamonds Mountain of Light, Sea of Light, and a large amount of gold. The peaceful result was that there was no bloodbath, no destruction, no unfair manipulation, and no upheaval of cultures. And that deep respect for each other pervades Indian-Iranian relations to this day for there is no conflict whatsoever between these two nations, and they remain mutually and spiritually bonded as neighbors right down to the present. Unfortunately, Iran subsequently was weakened militarily and politically after the death of Nāder Shāh and was unable to protect her Indian ally from the colonization and subjugation that was imposed upon India by England, who placed English governors over her sovereign territories. (Following independence from England, however, India has today become a much stronger democratic nation with industry and atomic capability despite the handicap of excessive population.)

Prior to this change of fortunes, a glance back at Persian history reveals what a strong moral and cultural background Iran inherited, which prevented them from ever being completely subdued, not even by such conquerors and occupiers as Alexander the Great, the fierce Mongols, nor the barbarian Arab hordes. Language and culture in Iran were always preserved because of the strength and backbone inherited from their Persian ancestors.

However, in 1979, the last vestige of hope was destroyed when England, France, and the United States, in their quest for control of oil, imposed the rule of a totally irresponsible mullah through a formulated coup d'etat. The clandestine goal of the West was to break the back and the spirit of this once mighty nation in order to more easily obtain the rich resource of oil with much less difficulty than if the imperial regime of Iran had maintained his rule over Iran. And since Iranians were anxious for greater freedom than the imperial Iranian government seemed willing to allow, they fell prey more readily to the subversion of the maneuvering of their Western "friends."

The vice president of the intelligence service of France flew to Baghdad on a specially monitored plane of Air France in order to bring Khomeini back to Paris to declare him the new leader of Iran. Meantime, the United States exerted its influence over the shah and forced him to leave Iran while England exercised its propaganda strategies in order to convince Iran and the rest of the world that the placement of Khomeini and his mullah henchmen would mean greater freedom and human rights for Iranians.

Whereas the United States of America dropped atomic bombs on Japan to end the great World War II conflict with the loss of thousands of lives, after less than fifty years, Hiroshima and Nagasaki have been restored, and the nation of Japan lives on. The destruction that has occurred in Iran because of the wrenching out of the heart of its culture has been much worse than the phenomenon that brought down the Japanese emperor, and much more will be required to restore the spirit of a people. Further insight into the effect of the events of 1979 upon my country are provided in my earlier book, *A Letter to Intellectuals*.

The aftermath of this cultural coup d'etat brought about by the West was eight years of a useless war between Iraq and Iran, the tragedy of 9/11, and the current imbroglio in Afghanistan and Iraq. All of these events have been accompanied by an inestimable loss of life and imponderable expenditure of money. My conclusion is that it is far better not to base foreign policy upon Sophist, Platonic, or Thrasymachian philosophy that denies the application of ethics, morality, or godliness to the treatment of strangers. The irony of such policy is that the people of those nations whose governments behave in such manner really approach their fellow human beings with attitudes of love, compassion, and kindness. A foreign policy derived from such philosophic tenets does not really represent the will of the people that the governmental leaders pretend to represent and contradicts their individual wishes. The vital interests of the people themselves call for love and concern for all people on this globe and not for their destruction or humiliation.

I also find it interesting that the same Western politicians attend church weekly, sing hymns, and chant God's praises just as do many of their fellow countrymen and women. But memory is short, and what they profess on Sunday is forgotten in their global activities and actions on Monday. It is also my conclusion that foreign policy that is based on lies, deception, and subjugation will never be successful as a working agenda for any nation.

And once again, I emphasize what I know is fact; viz, the people of Iran have absolutely no interest in having an aggressive encounter or in putting down the culture of any other country or group of people. The Iranian spirit is derived from a noble Persian tradition of truth, love, and respect for others and a peaceful regard for all who inhabit this planet. Iran has always had an admiration for the United States, for Israel, for Russia, for Palestine, and for all the rest of this world. The current imposed Islamic regime does not in any way truly represent the love for harmony that characterizes Iranian culture!

Chapter Six

Religion: The Jews, Islam Roots, and Teaching

Thousands of years before Christ (twenty-second century BC), as described in Genesis chapter twelve, Abraham covenanted with God and was the founder of a monotheistic faith. He was a friend of God's, and he was a wealthy man. Eventually, he had two sons—Ishmael, issue of Hagar, his wife's handmaid, and a product of human planning; and Isaac, issue of Sara, his wife, and a product of God's grace. Through these two offspring, there developed two major branches of religious practices: the nation of the Hebrew religion through Isaac, and the nation of Islam through the person of Ishmael. In short, both of these important expressions of religious faith, Hebrew and Muslim, stem from one man and father—Abraham. And both are faiths that emphasize law with definite ways of carrying out acts of worship and tune manner of daily living.

In a sort of contemporary religious expression (600 BC), Zoroastrians advised all people to think, to imagine, and to behave well; they were to speak truthfully and clearly. They believed that all human beings have both good and evil within themselves, and they urged that individuals emphasize the positive or good impulse within them rather than the negative or evil side. And interestingly, Zoroaster was also a monotheist, ascribing all good to

Ahura Mazda but acknowledging the continuous struggle of good with evil. Although there were guiding principles whereby life was to be lived, worship and society were not a tedious prescription of ways in which to do things, but more a spontaneous outpouring of the good within each individual. With special respect for fire and sun as symbols of knowledge and God, the Iranians celebrate the first day of winter (December 21), Yalda, as the first of the longest nights in the year, which some believe to be the birth of sunlight and the Wise Men interpreted to be the birth of Jesus. This attitude toward life sort of foreshadowed the principle of love as the motive for living for the Christian rather than "doing because the law says so" as is the underlying rhythm of Jew and Muslim.

A major emphasis of the Hebrew faith is their salvation from enslavement under the Egyptians. In spite of this key motif, Moses, affected as he was by his Egyptian upbringing, readily accepted ideals and principles of his Egyptian ancestry and adopted the wisdom of Egypt's sages as the basis for the extensive legislation recorded in the Pentateuch. And throughout its pages is a basic undercurrent of doing justice for it is in this life, not in a heaven of reward, that being fair plays out its effects and determines the type of existence that men and women will either enjoy or abhor.

In summary then, the origin of Hebrew law derives from three sources: the first being that of Egyptian influence, the second being Babylonian (the Code of Hammurabi), and the third being of natural or basic Semitic tribal tradition. As already suggested, salvation from enslavement in Egypt prompted the Mosaic aspect of Hebrew legal process whereas the later captivity in Babylon led to the permeation of Cyrus the Great and the Hammurabic principles into Jewish forensics. Desert wanderings and the Canaanite environment molded a third portion of the all-important principles of living (e.g., the Ten Commandments). Modifications were inevitable. Whereas "an eye for an eye, a tooth for a tooth" was graded for the Mesopotamians according to class or wealth, for the Jew, the principle applied universally and without class distinction. And even in Hebrew codification, there was some discrimination between the Jew and the stranger. For example, when someone works for a master, the owner pays more for the Hebrew slave than for the foreigner; and a Hebrew slave might be freed without ransom after seven years whereas the immigrant slave was released only with a price to be paid. In general, there is love and compassion for the poor, the widowed, and the downtrodden in principle although the omission of that concern by the dominant was the rallying point of the prophets throughout biblical history.

Returning to Islam, the wandering clan (Arab) that originated through Ishmael, bastard offspring of Abraham and Hagar, was certainly Hebrew in origin. Thus, Arab history was initiated long before the birth of the Islam in (AD 610). This period of Arab existence before Islam is referred to as the "ignorant" period, and very little information exists concerning this phase of Arab history except for some poetry. These poems are characterized by boasting about family and tribal origin. Examples are "Bani Tamim," "Ady," and "Bani Hashem."

Such poetry is the only extant information from that period; and it seems that there was no other expression—such as mathematics, philosophy, or science—preserved for our understanding. Thus, genealogical superiority defined the standing of an individual.

We do know also that during this period, a woman was of no importance whatsoever. If the issue of a pregnancy was female, the shame upon the father was so great that often he would bury the offspring alive. Because of this practice, there were too few women to satisfy all the males, so one woman might have to be the consort of many men, and she would enjoy no individuality nor have any rights. And there was no limitation upon the number of wives a man might have, provided he could find an available woman.

Usually, different tribes were fighting one another, and if a man was unable to carry out his revenge upon a member of another clan during his lifetime, he would leave in his will that his offspring should effect that deed. Should he actually have a feeling of goodwill toward another clan, he often would will that his successors should act kindly toward that other group.

Conflict was the theme of the times, but fortunately, there was a period of about three or four months each year when fighting was forbidden. Next to pride in his cohort of tribal members was a man's love and devotion to his camel. Since there was very little to read or to read about, most individuals on the Arabian Peninsula were illiterate. Probably no more than five individuals among the primarily sheepherders were able to read. And idol worship was rampant. All of the Arabian Peninsula and Yemen were under Persian control.

It was into this rather bleak set of circumstances that Mohammed was born in about AD 570. He came into a tribe that was the most famous and powerful governing clan in Mecca. His kinsmen were known as Koreish, and they were the overseers of the Kaaba, which was the first altar built by Abraham in gratitude to his one god although it had become a shrine devoted to many idols. Mecca had become a center to which tribes in the peaceful months brought their idols, and it quite naturally had also become the chief site for commerce and trade, primarily of spices. In spite of that, the territory around Mecca was so poor that Persia had relieved its inhabitants of the duty of paying taxes.

Students of Arab history believe that it was only because of Mohammed's birth into the Koreish that circumstances allowed him to become considered to be a prophet. Mohammed's father had died before he was born (AD 570), and his mother had succumbed before he reached the age of six years. His grandfather Abdul Muttalib, who was highly respected by the Koreish tribe, became his guardian upon the death of his dad; and finally, Mohammed's uncle Abū Ṭālib succeeded his grandfather in his guardianship following the death of the elder gentleman. This succession of relatives provided Mohammed with excellent protection during his jejune days, and he experienced no threats from outsiders. In fact, from the very start, Mohammed was known for his fine character. He was renowned for his trustworthiness, reliability, honesty, faithfulness, and rectitude. When he had reached his twentieth birthday, he was termed Mohammed Amein, meaning "the trusted one." At about that time, a very wealthy widow named Khadijah, thought to be a Christian, became interested in Mohammed; her uncle was Ebne-Arkam, a respected scholar of the Bible and one who also was known as a Christian. Although Khadijah (forty years old) was twice the age of Mohammed, they eventually married, and he came in to her employ and traveled often to Syria in this relationship. During these travels, Mohammed met many individuals of different cultures and religious beliefs, especially representatives of Jewish, Christian, and the Zoroastrian traditions.

Mohammed, in addition to his sterling character, was a genius and had keen insight into the fact that his territory and tribe were not in very good shape. He decided to initiate a revolution in order to overthrow the government in his native city of Mecca. Now the Koreish tribe originated from Abd Manaf, who had two sons, Umayya and Hashim (the sons of Umayya are called Banu Umayyad; the sons of Hashim are called Banu Hashim—Mohammed was from Banu Hashim).

Umayya was the governor of Mecca and was uneducated, a Fascist, and a fanatic—as was his following among the population. Mohammed, who was part of Banu Hashim intensely keen on becoming governor in Umayya's place, was quite the opposite of Umayya and was well acquainted with the management of people through his business experience. He was extremely persuasive and quite knowledgeable in dealing with the differences of individuals, easily convincing them of the wisdom of his enterprising ways. Many of Mecca's inhabitants at that time were extremely unhappy with existing conditions and the religion; and following that, Mohammed soon created an organized system of faith and worship—Islam, which stems from the word *islaf* (forward purchase, trade, or business).

In Arabic, the declination of termination of contract is *aslafa, yoselefo, islaf* as in "He forward purchases," "He'll forward purchase," "To forward purchase"; by substituting an *m* for *f*, according to Arabic grammar and syntax, the words *aslamah, yoselemo,* and "Islam" come to mean "He forward purchases," "He will forward purchase," or "To forward purchase." Thus, "Islam" means a purchase ahead of time or for the future. In short, "Islam" means a future or forward purchase, which essentially suggests a trade or purchase with payment well in advance. It is understood that the buyer in this circumstance accepts the payment as a completed deal, without any right of annulment or any redress. In the context of the religious practices, a Muslim pays a tithe or other alms (according to one's wealth) toward support of the poor "ahead of time" as a requirement for membership in the Islamic profession of faith. A number of illustrations of the manifestation of this membership prerequisite will be provided at a later time.

We follow a somewhat similar line of reasoning in coming to an understanding of the word "Allah" in the Arabic vocabulary. The word derives from *alahah*, *yaleho*, and *elahh* meaning "He bows down," "He'll bow down," or "To bow down." Thus, Allah is a master or deity before whom we prostrate ourselves. Allah is master of all, and we are slaves to this superior being. Next to him, we have no personal rights at all, and he is to be worshiped. People are to obey Allah and his prophets. Practical application of this obedience is monetary tribute: one pays 5 percent to Allah and to his prophet; and there is a very specific scale of payment in terms of grain, camels, food animals, gold, and silver.

The god (Allah) of Islam is kind and compassionate, but at times, he may be very angry.

He may even be in a rage or furious! If a person tries to trick or deceive Allah, that person will experience even more the much greater trickery and deceit put forth by an angered Allah. The Koran states that if an individual is willing to trade his or her life for the sake of Allah, then they may go straight to heaven; the killing of oneself for the sake of Allah never results in bankruptcy or a failed market. Another verse of the Koran states that if a believer prays every day, fasts regularly, pays his or her tithe, encourages others to do the right thing, and discourages others from wrongdoing, then they are assured of prosperity in this life and in heaven in the next.

Allah says, "We create you as man and woman, we create you as a tribe or nation, and we want you to know that those who observe virtue and abstinence are more honorable than those who do not."

And according to the code of Islam, Muslims and non-Muslims are not created equal; a Muslim is of much more worth. And a Muslim must be kind and compassionate toward other Muslims while he or she must be strict or severe with non-Muslims.

Also, men and women are not equal; only one-third of inheritance goes to the female survivors while two-thirds of inheritance goes to the remaining male offspring. Furthermore, in instances of court decisions, the testimony of a woman is worth only one-half that of a man, and the sworn statements of four women or only of two men are necessary to establish the acceptability of an issue in question. When a Muslim kills another Muslim, there is a fine of one hundred camels (or its equivalent) that the perpetrator of the act must pay the family; but if a Muslim kills a woman, then the fine to be paid the family is only fifty camels (or its equivalent).

The substance of the above paragraphs is to demonstrate the supreme authority of Allah according to the Muslim faith and to point out some, but hardly all, of the discriminating statements that are made in the Koran concerning male and female as well Muslims and non-Muslims. Our attention will be focused next upon the expansion and growth in numbers of Mohammedans throughout the present-day world.

As has been pointed out before, the origins of both Hebrew and Muslim religions and their languages, which share much in common, are from the same root. The gods of each discriminate between members of their faith and those who are outside the faith. The Hebrew god, Elohim, gave to his people a special land in which to dwell viz, Canaan, whereas the god of Islam, Allah, promised heaven to his followers, a joy that those who are not Muslim are not allowed to experience. Muslims also believe that Kaaba, the first Eben-Ezer erected by Abraham and located in Mecca, is the home of Allah. Every Muslim who can afford it is obliged to make a pilgrimage to Kaaba in Mecca at least once in his or her lifetime, and all Muslims are required to face toward Mecca during daily prayer.

The Hammurabic code is the basic principle of both Islamic and Jewish law; so "an eye for an eye, a tooth for a tooth, and a life for a life" is inherent in the creeds of both faiths. Therefore, there is no forgiveness, and revenge is the driving motive in human relationships. This principle makes it very difficult to solve the differences that exist today between Israel and Palestine inasmuch as forgiveness is not the modus operandi.

Reviewing a little bit, what is the foremost belief of Islam? The proper response is that "Allah is the one and only existing God." There is one small portion or confession of the Koran known as the sura Tohid, which means "God is one." Every time a Mohammedan prays, and that must be done five times a day, he or she must include this confession, either at the beginning or ending of his or her prayer. It may be translated as "Mohammed, tell the people that Allah is one. Allah is without needs. Allah is not born from any person nor is any person born from him. There is no one equal to him!" Such is the sura Tohid.

There is a second confession that one must also make in daily prayer; this is the Nobovat, which means "124,000 prophets and messengers, starting with Adam and ending with Mohammed." These special prophets or messengers may or may not have written a book, and some are evangelists for the whole world or just for some smaller area of the world. Acknowledgment of these special individuals must be made in each prayer.

A third confession must also be mentioned in each prayer for it also is a basic Muslim belief. It is entitled Maa'de and means "resurrection." It is the assertion that each individual is promised that he or she will return to the earth after death in a restored body.

Of such is the basic Muslim creed; and each adherent of Islam must accept these beliefs, whether Sunni or Shiites, and reiterate these confessions in daily prayer. One who is a Shiite Muslim, however, has two additional required confessions to make. These are known as Adle and Imamat. Adle simply states that Allah is just and never unjust. Imamat is encumbered with far more repercussions but refers basically to a belief that when Mohammed died, he appointed Imam Ali as his successor and that each subsequent successor has the right to name his successor of which, according to the Shiite branch of Islam, there are twelve Imams. The twelfth Imam, who continues to rule since he has never died and who cannot be seen until such time as Allah, in his good providence, wills that he does appear. As one retired professor from Muskingum College (New Concord, Ohio), a Dr. Herb Thomson, once said to me, "So many superstitions exist in Islam, but those who are Shiite have extra superstitions." The Shiites believe that Mohammed and Fatimah, his daughter, and the subsequent twelve Imams constitute a body of individuals, fourteen in number, who are without sin.

In general, those who specialize in the study of the Islamic faith believe that it is a religion of sword and of means. The Shiites themselves attribute the success of Islam to three basic phenomena: (1) the wealth of Mohammed's wife Khadijah; (2) the sword of Imam Ali, Mohammed's chosen successor; and (3) the perseverance of Mohammed himself. The scholars of Islam, however, perceive that if Mohammed had been from some tribe like Rabieh, Adie, Batoon, or any tribe other than Koreish, then he most likely could never have survived or have been a success for the influence of the tribe of Koreish was indeed very great, almost beyond imagining. And as already stated several times, Mohammed belonged to that very unique tribe

In AD 622, Mohammed fled from Mecca to Yathrib (later named Medina) because many in Mecca who were worshiping idols and not one god, Allah, were severely criticized by him and so formed a group who planned to murder him. Mohammed fled in the dark of night to Yathrib where he soon became governor of that area. And it was because he had belonged to the tribe of Koreish that he was greeted with great respect, most especially by two Jewish tribes, Aus and Khazraj, who long had been at each other's throats but who, because they both sought Mohammed's favor, were brought together into a peaceful relationship by this escapee from Mecca. As the new governor of Medina, he built it into a mighty military power; and after eight years of governance, he returned to Mecca in AD 630 and forced it into submission through three major encounters known as Badr, Ohud, and Khaibar. Victorious in these three conflicts, Mohammed became the ruler of Mecca, and all the chiefs of the tribe of Koreish bowed down to and feared the sword of Mohammed. For example, one such leader, Abu Sufyan, was approached by an emissary of Mohammed and was ordered to accept Islam. He added, "If you, Abu Sufyan, do not accept Islam, I will cut your head off at the neck with this sword."

Abu Sufyan replied to Mohammed's envoy, "I do."

At which point, the emissary retorted, "Then repeat after me, 'I confess that Allah is one!'" which response was quickly made by Abu Sufyan. Finally, Mohammed's representative demanded that Abu Sufyan declare that "Mohammed is the messenger of Allah."

When Abu Sufyan refused, saying, "This is very hard for me for my heart cannot accept this," the envoy told him that he should look behind him and see that there were eleven thousand men with swords. "All your uncle's sons, ready to kill you," Abu Sufyan relented and reiterated that such was very hard for him to do, but because "I am afraid for my life, I am ready to say, 'Mohammed is the messenger of God,' but to say these words is as if I am taking bitter poison.'"

By just such incidents, Mohammed was established as the governor and representative of Allah as well in Mecca as in Medina. His indeed was a power difficult to challenge, especially as the messenger of Allah. A case in point and one that illustrates the mastery accomplished through his role as messenger of Allah. Some of the city of Mecca no longer remained under the governance of Umayya because Mohammed, as the messenger of Allah, declared an end to the rule of Abd Manaf, Umayya's other son, and placed Hashim in charge from his distant government seat in Medina.

However, at the height of his political career, Mohammed underwent a distinct change in his moral character. Whereas formerly he had embraced kindness, mercy, and generosity, he now became much more ruthless and demanding. His more ruthless nature exerted itself when he ordered all idols in the Kaaba to be destroyed. Back in Mecca, Umayya had no choice but to submit to the whim of Mohammed; but he awaited a later opportunity to oppose Mohammed, a subterfuge that Mohammed was aware of. Much later, Mohammed invited all his closest companions to the Ghadir Khumm where he made the recommendation that Ali, his son-in-law, was to be his successor to the leadership. This suggestion was not followed however; and at the time of Mohammed's death, it was generally agreed that Abū Bakr, Mohammed's father-in-law and his companion when he fled Mecca to Medina, should be his successor. Ali accepted this consensus opinion and cooperated with Abū Bakr.

Following the death of Mohammed, Islam, which largely had been limited to the areas around Mecca and Medina, began to expand outside of the Arabian Peninsula. There also had been no Koran save for some portions that had been indicated in the memories of a few faithful followers. Inasmuch as the imposition of Islam by Mohammed had been accomplished by force, those who succeeded him decided to enlarge the influence of Islam by the same forceful means. Inasmuch as there was a lot of injustice and persecution in the Persian and Roman provinces when the new faith promised a glimmer of hope for those seeking to escape this unjust oppression, they quickly embraced this alternate expression of religious fervor. In less than two decades following the death of Mohammed, Islam spread to Syria (AD 625), Iraq (AD 637), Palestine and to the remainder of the Persian Empire (AD 640) and Egypt (AD 642).

In actuality, Islam has continued to enlarge its numbers throughout history. At present, Islam continues to grow; so throughout the world, its membership now numbers over 1.3 billion. Such tremendous growth, yet in fact, Islam did not introduce anything new or different to its growing following; more particularly, as a faith with widespread adherence, it really did nothing to improve their lives or society. An ancient Persian proverb declares in Farsi that "Your roots are Arab, and you are from root, Arab," implying that nothing has changed even if Islam is your newfound basic belief. Your allegiance to Islam does not mean that you really and deeply understood anything new at all (in dwelling upon this vapidity, I do not mean to offend the Arab intelligence but am merely attempting to clarify the situation).

Omar was the second successor to Mohammed at the death of Abū Bakr. When he was informed of the discovery at Madaeen of a number of Persian texts dealing with mathematics, science, medicine, and astronomy and when asked what should be done with these new revelations of wisdom, he replied that since there was no better understanding that exists in the world than that which exists in the Koran and it alone is sufficient for us, then we have no need of any other source of knowledge and to burn these newly discovered books. My point is that not only did Islam not introduce any new thing to the progress of this planet's society at its early inception, but that it actually destroyed and set back the advancement of mankind!

The historian Tabari underscores the fact that it was the oppression of the king of Persia that his subjects were seeking to escape that permitted the Arabs to convert so many Iranians to Islam and to defeat the nation's superiorly armed might. Had the Persians not suspended their resistance in the hope of a better way out, the Arabs would not have conquered Persia, which, indeed, was the superpower of that time. In fact, it was a hollow victory, and the Arab Muslims are foolishly proud of "their victory of victories."

(In all of this, there may be a lesson for the United States, today's superpower. Just as the Persians let down their guard in the hope of overcoming inequities permitted by their leader, if the United States does not continue to resist al Qaeda and Hezbollah with a superior morality and attention to just treatment, it also might be dethroned from its position of leadership. We cannot allow arrogance and pride to cause us to ignore the lessons that are found in attention to history! Let us take heed and rule with justice, love, and compassion rather than debase ourselves because of fear and misplaced regard for honesty and fairness!)

There is a book entitled *Twenty Three Years: A Study of the Prophetic Career of Mohammad*; it refers to twenty-three years of Mohammed as a prophet or messenger of Allah. It was written by famous contemporary author Ali Dashti. He studied Islam in Najaf, Iraq, and was a member of the parliament of Iran. Later, he became a senator and was eventually appointed during the imperial regime of Iran as ambassador to Lebanon. It is of interest that when Khomeini came to power, Ali Dashti was arrested and questioned because of this writing even though he had not officially claimed to be its author. The new Islamic regime knew, nonetheless, that he had published it as a book and that he was its author. Also, significant is the fact that anyone who was discovered to have this book in his or her possession was brought to court, questioned, and had his or her life placed in jeopardy.

In the book *Twenty Three Years*, Ali Dashti stated several provocative ideas. First, he reiterated the concept that the Islamic faith did not bring any new or beneficial principle to society except possibly for hajj (pilgrimage to Mecca) and jihad (war with kafirs or nonbelievers). He clearly asserted that everything taught in Islam had already been stated in writing in Hebrew (Talmud or Old Testament), Christianity (New Testament), or the Zend Avesta (Zoroastrian holy text). He also indicated that there is some Bedouin tradition incorporated into Islam.

Second, Ali Dashti questioned how the Shiites could claim that Mohammed was a sinless person. He pointed out that when Mohammed defeated Mecca, he had killed one individual by his own hand even though his victim had pleaded for mercy and the sparing of his life. Not heeding the imploring of this man, Mohammed took his life anyway (both Sunnis and Shiites have confirmed this incident).

Furthermore, the relationships of Mohammed to his fourteen wives suggest at least a little human fallibility for Mohammed spent a different night with each of these members of his harem. (The circumstance is described in Surat At-Tahrim, a chapter of the Koran.) One such night, when it was the turn for Aisha and while she had absented herself from bed to prepare food for Mohammed, he unexpectedly encountered her maid and had sexual relations with her instead of Aisha.

Unknown to Mohammed, Aisha entered the room and quickly assessed the situation. When Aisha scolded him for what he had done, he apologized, asked her not to share the story with any of the others, and promised not to do such a thing again. On a later occasion, however, the incident was repeated. Aisha again scolded Mohammed and asked why he had broken his promise. Again, Mohammed apologized but explained that he had not wanted to repeat his heinous unfaithful action but that the angel Gabriel had come from Allah and asked him why he should regard something to be unlawful when, after all, he, as master of his domain, should not consider it unlawful to lie with any woman in his household. So the angel of Allah had convinced him of the propriety of his permissive behavior. In short, his defense was that Allah had led him to the salacious action; so all was acceptable, and he was not to be blamed.

Another questionable occasion is described in Surat al-Ahzab, verse 36. The incident is related in this manner: "One day, Mohammed saw the wife of his close friend, and he liked her very much! Later, another friend told Mohammed's close friend that since Mohammed loves your wife, you must divorce her so that Mohammed, who is the messenger of God, can marry her. There is nothing wrong with this!" Apparently, this was the course of action followed; and Ali Dashti, who was advised by an interpreter of the Koran, related how this close friend—in spite of his great love for his wife, and she for him—eventually set his wife aside so Mohammed could proceed to marry her.

There is a different version of this last incident, which was explained by Mahmud al-Aghad, an Egyptian specialist in the subject of Islam who eventually came to the United States and became a U.S. citizen. He was a prolific writer about Islam and finally lost his life along with sixty others in the bombing by al Qaeda of a large hotel in Amman, the capitol of Jordan. His description went like this: Mohammed had no son at all (in Arabic, anyone who has no son is known as *abtar*, which means "no tail"), so he adopted Zayd ibn Harithah. He arranged the marriage of this adopted youth to his uncle's daughter whose name was Zainab. This turned out to be the woman whom he saw and liked, so he forced his adopted son to divorce her so he might marry her. According to Arabic law, a father-in-law cannot marry his son's wife. Mohammed, however, insisted that he had not broken the law since his son was adopted; and the law speaks only in regard to a son by birth, not by adoption.

Commenting upon all of these connubial shenanigans, Ali Dashti raised the question in his book *Twenty Three Years* of how we can possibly endorse the claim of the Shiites that Mohammed was sinless. Sheik Haidar Isfafahani, who was a religious teacher in Najaf, Iraq, said, "I personally would also like to point out that since Mohammed did not have a son or grandson through his adopted son nor any direct offspring whatsoever, how can so many of the Shiite sect claim to relate themselves to Mohammed as their grandfather?" Such Shiites call themselves Sayed and distinguish themselves from all other Muslims by wearing a black (sometimes green) turban. This allows them special social recognition, and they are eligible to receive an alms tithe from their peers; and sinners among them never go to hell, but they go to the Zamharier—intense cold, no heavy punishment for Sayed.

Unfortunately, there is a great deal of exaggeration among the Shiites. To accomplish questionable ends, many invalid stories are concocted and special favors expected. For example, once, Imam Ali in the Nohravan war in Iraq declared before the war started, "I swear to Allah that among the enemy (our foes), all of them will be killed except ten of them will not be killed, and even ten of us will not be killed." After the war, his predictions were recognized as having been confirmed, so a group of people promoted him and declared that he was the same as God. They called themselves Ali-Allahi, which stood for "Ali is Allah" and encouraged gullible Shiite peers to join them. As a result, many people came to Imam, bowed down to him, and declared that he was the same as Allah. In his modesty and rectitude, he insisted that he was not any such divinity and stated, "No, I came from dust just like anyone else, and I will return to dust!"

From my own standpoint, when I was in graduate school in a class devoted to study of Islam here in the United States, I had a professor whom, for the sake of anonymity, I will call Fits. He was quite knowledgeable about the Muslim faith and about the Arabic language. During one of his lectures about Islam, I mentioned Ali Dashti and his book *Twenty Three Years*. The professor indicated that he was familiar with it and added the following, "With respect, I must even refute what Ali Dashti had to say concerning hajj and jihad for I feel that Islam did not even contribute these entities to society for there are many instances of both in the Old Testament." He indicated that many are the instances of wars and pilgrimages in the annals of the scriptures, but of course, "Mohammed demanded that those with money make a journey to Mecca instead of Jerusalem as the Hebrews had for that was a matter of 'good business practices' to have a site of attraction on the Arabian Peninsula." He continued, "Therefore, what Islam brought to this old planet were no new ideas at all, notwithstanding the two items suggested by Ali Dashti!"

Professor Fits also commented that according to the Sura Asra, Mohammed did not perform any miracles. He added that this portion of the Koran also explains that when Moses and Jesus did perform miracles, many people denied these feats; so Mohammed excused himself by suggesting that if he were to have performed miracles, they also would have been denied, so why the bother of trying such actions? This prompted me (there were two other students from the Middle East who had studied Islam in al-Azhar University in Cairo) to ask a question, "If the Koran is a permanent miracles guide according to all Muslim belief and if the verses of the Koran say that Allah spoke to Mohammed and told him to say to all humans and jinns that even if they get together and cooperate with each other, they would not ever be able to bring into existence anything like this holy book, how is it that we have this marvelous text to refer to?"

At this, the professor asked if I was from Iran, to which query I responded positively. Then professor responded, "No one in this world can reproduce the complete works of Hāfez from the city of Shiraz. And similarly, no one can reproduce the complete works of Shakespeare. Further, no one can produce the works of al-Mutanabbi that he wrote in Arabic. Now because these works that I have mentioned cannot be reproduced because of the ingenious qualities, does that make them miraculous?" Ali Dashti added in his book also that according to Arabic grammar, there are some grammatical mistakes used in the Koran. However, following this response, the three of us left the classroom and were quite upset.

The next day, the professor commented further, "I am here to explain, without any bias, everything intellectually and to explore actual facts. At the same time, I respect the faith of everyone in this class and in the world. I have no intention of offending anyone." However, in the next breath, he posed this thought to the class. "Every year, there are about more than a million wealthy individuals from all over the world who make a pilgrimage to Mecca and perform numerous religious rituals and ceremonies. Has there been any benefit to all the other poor and needy members of the Muslim faith as a result of these pilgrimages performed by those who have journeyed from so many distant parts of the world? If so, please explain these changes for the better of me and show me if the ones who have been the travelers have demonstrated any remarkable alteration in their behavior or if they have become individuals who are more helpful, more truthful, compassionate, or kind." This further reflection seemed to leave us with a feeling that the professor's attitude toward Muslim practices had a somewhat pejorative outlook in spite of proclaimed absence of bias.

In reference to jihad, some further considerations are in order. First, today we have al Qaeda and Hezbollah who are fighting against the Western powers. They justify this action since they are fighting with kafir *harbi*, anyone who is not a Muslim. *Harbi* means those who are at war with the Muslim faith or any group or individual who is supportive of those who are at war with Muslims. For example, Islam has declared that Israel is a warring enemy, thus a kafir. Any nation supportive of Israel, such as the United States of America, therefore, is considered kafir *harbi* as in any other country in that situation. Russia and China, neither of which are supporters of Israel, are considered kafirs, but not kafir *harbi*; and this allows Islam to consider these two countries as potential friends. Should they additionally become helpful in fighting against kafir *harbi*, they will also be eligible to be financially compensated out of religiously collected tithes as a bonus for their support of Islam.

One ordinary Arab, Sheik Abdul-al-Montakem (name means "servant of revenger Allah) is very outspoken and directs this comment to the Western powers, "If you are asleep, wake up. If you are drunk, get sober. You should know that since Israel is a kafir *harbi* and has seized and occupied Palestine, which is Islamic Arab territory and not Israel's. This situation dictates that Muslims must directly or indirectly fight with Israel!"

Further example, Osama bin Laden and the Taliban are confronting Israel directly as the occupier of Palestine whereas the king of Saudi Arabia, the president of Egypt, as well as the sheiks of Kuwait, United Arab Emirates, Qatar, and Bahrain are opposing Israel indirectly by sharing their technological, financial, and intelligence capabilities with al Qaedan Islam through unpublicized channels directed against the West. Their relative positions of weakness certainly prevent them from opposing these powers openly, and by participating in the struggle secretly, they are fulfilling their religious obligations without being subject to monitoring or condemnation. In addition, the world must know the facts that the existence of Israel in Palestine was for the reason that Palestine was a colony of England.

Another example of how the fervor of Islamists is related to their bellicosity is supplied by an incident in the past when an undercover CIA officer in Afghanistan who looked exactly like a resistance fighter of the mujahedeen (clothes, beard, and turban) grabbed an antiaircraft missile weapon and fired at a Russian aircraft. When the enemy helicopter plunged to the ground, the impersonator raised his weapon into the air, shot with it, and shouted, "Allah-ho-akbar," which means "Allah is greater than everything else." No one could imagine that this individual was not a member of the Afghan mujahedeen, and his reaction was entirely fitting of that role, a kafir *harbi*.

The fortunes of war often involve a reversal of roles and strange bedfellows as kafir *harbi*. The USA could not win in Vietnam because of the part played by Communist China and the former Soviet Union in their undercover support of the Vietnamese. Later, the former Soviet Union found themselves in a similar position in Afghanistan; they were without any chance of gaining victory or even the smallest inroad in that country because of the clandestine support of the West for that Eastern neighbor of Iran. Eventually, they withdrew their effort to change the political climate of Afghanistan but not without having tasted the bitterness of significant loss of human life and financial devastation. In this circumstance, the Afghan Muslims attributed their victory entirely to the persistence of the mujahedeen yet completely overlooking crucial help supplied by the West as kafir *harbi*. The promulgation of Osama bin Laden and his cause was an irony of this situation already mentioned.

As previously mentioned, the result of the military occupation of Iraq is the death of large numbers of young men and women of the USA and allied Western nations, far in excess of the innocents who died on 9/11, and the maiming and destruction of thousands of civilian Iraqis. The supposed friends of the United States in the Middle East, such as Saudi Arabia and Egypt, perceive this conflict to be for the purpose of stabilizing the security of Israel and to acquire better access to oil, not to promote democracy and human rights. The real intention of these Middle Eastern nations is kafir harbi, not to allow the United States or its Western supporters to overpower and occupy them and to do so without being recognized or detected. The Taliban and al Qaeda consider this subterfuge as a victory for Islam; so even if the Taliban and Osama bin Laden are destroyed, just as Saddam Hussein and Zarqawi were eliminated, it will not affect the outcome of this struggle very much nor bring about victory for the United States or its allies. Beyond such events, even if they were to occur, there would remain over one billion three hundred thousand Muslims, among whom are so many extremists dedicated to killing themselves and killing kafirs that they need not rely upon the stance of their individual unidentified persons with extremist intentions that security measures could never round up or isolate them before they could carry out their destructive ends.

With this grim picture in mind, is it truly feasible to consider victory in Iraq or Afghanistan, or can one really consider that the status of Israel is more secure by virtue of the fighting in Iraq? Is there actually any justification realistic for carrying on these military actions? For what justifiable reason can families continue to lose beloved members, and for what achievable purpose can the war be continued? Can the lies and deception of foreign policy based upon Sophism and Platonic intransigence solve the bigger problem? Do we continue to justify evil for evil? I reiterate the words of Sheik Montakem, "If you are asleep, wake up! If you are drunk, get sober!" Let us not continue to play games and politics with the lives of human beings.

Returning again to the subject of the seventh-century war between the Arabs and Iran, the reason for the eventual defeat of superior Iran by the relative nomads was the internal corruption of the leadership of Iran and its mistreatment of Iranian citizens at that time. These Iranian subjects were looking for a way out of their downtrodden existence, so they were disinclined to stand up for the miserable oppressors who were treating them so badly. At that time, the people of Iran were under the dictatorship of the Sassanid dynasty; and they were suffering extreme torture, tyranny, and injustice. There was no possibility of resisting the subjugation that they were experiencing. The leaders of the Zoroastrian religious sect, known as magi or moghan, were subservient to the king; so that they had little concern for the needs of the hoi polloi. Their very magi concurred with whatever orders came from the throne, and all injustices and inequities were ignored. Because of this very unhealthy and dire situation, the people were praying for a savior of some sort.

Finally, due to these circumstances, one bold Iranian, Salman al-Farsi, absented himself from Iran and traveled to Mecca in Saudi Arabia in order to examine the religious fervor that was emanating from that holy city. His unique presence in Mecca allowed him to become a close personal friend of Mohammed. His intellectual capability permitted him to lend great assistance to his newly established friend and to the entire Muslim cause. In little time, Mohammed began to refer to Farsi as a member of his family and to treat him with great deference. Mohammed is quoted in Arabic as saying, "Al-Salmaano menaa ahlol bait," which established the Iranian as kith and kin.

Circumstances for Iranians back then in the seventh-century AD might be likened to the situation of a person who is drowning in a stormy sea. Such an unfortunate grasps for any object that might come into sight in order to save himself or herself from drowning, grasping for straws in order to preserve the possibility of having one's life spared. The point that I, again, am attempting to make is that life in the superpower Iran in those desolate days of the seventh-century AD was so intolerable that the soldiers of the king could not justify fighting for a king who was so corrupt and tyrannical that his victory would only prolong their misery and that of the Iranian citizenry. Thus, these soldiers had no reason to fight with any enthusiasm, and they reflected their hopelessness and displeasure by failing to try to resist the invading Arab hordes. They even refused to employ the elephants that had been trained to kill the enemy, and eventually, Iran fell to the underdog intruding Bedouins. The Arabs overthrew the political might of superpower Iran, but never could kill the resurgent pride of a people who had once been a revered and respected Persian Empire. One proof of that is the fact that the Arabic language never replaced the native tongue of Iran (Farsi or Persian), and unlike in other surrounding Middle Eastern kingdoms defeated by the Arabs like Egypt, Lebanon, Palestine, West Africa, etc., the Persian language has always remained the mother tongue—even to this day! For a hundred years, Iranians were forced to have the Arabic language in formal schools as per the government's administration.

When, in 1979, the Western powers conspired to overthrow a ruling Iranian dynasty, the hypocrisy and thievery of the Islamic Khomeini, who was placed in power, was so completely damning to the soul of the nation that its spirit was broken and that the upheaval far outweighed the effect of their defeat by the Arabs centuries earlier. For the Iranian nation, the downfall in the twentieth century was far more destructive to the culture of its people. I reiterate that when Khomeini came to power, he cancelled all projects with the outside world, including the building of an atomic-fueled power plant with the assistance of Germany amounting to eight hundred million dollars and a uranium-enrichment facility cosponsored by France. Iran had actually prepaid the French two billion dollars at that time toward this last project and was refunded only one billion at the time of its cancellation. He also closed all the universities of Iran and executed by hanging and decapitation all highly educated military and civilian leaders. More than three million scholars had no choice but to flee their country in order to escape imprisonment and death. Many of the Iranians in 1979 were demonstrating for freedom, certainly not for Khomeini or Islam, but they were joined by all other groups opposing the rule of the shah such as the Communists, the Nationalists, and the Islamic mujahedeen. In no way could any of these more radical groups have overcome the shah; but by uniting together with those seeking freedom, their influence became an overwhelming force that, together with subverting Western elements, brought about his downfall. Whatever, the integrity of the nation was destroyed by the cooperation of a misguided leadership alliance who were expressing their displeasure with the status quo rather than any real preference for the whacks mullah who replaced him!*

My conclusion is that in order to maintain the safety of a nation, it is necessary that its leadership provide its citizens with equitable governance and that this same justice be extended to all other nations with whom relations are maintained. It is also well to pursue peaceful ends rather than to make a display of regimental and military might. The effectiveness and power of love and compassion are inestimable.

So many Islamic historians believe that the intellectual leaders of their faith never completely converted to the revengeful tenets of the religion and that, in the bottom of their souls, they only gave verbal acquiescence to these more arrogant doctrines in order to save their lives. For example, following the defeat of Iran by Islam when Omar, second successor to Mohammed, said to Hormozan, governor of Khuzestan, "Accept Islam, or I will cut your neck!"

The response of Hormozan was, "I do not accept Islam, so cut my neck!" As his Islamic tormentors readied to cut his head off, he further added, "Give me one glass of water to drink before executing me for I want to be assured that I may drink this glass of water before they cut my neck." The Islamic caliph presiding before the court filled with observing people assured Hormozan that he would not behead him before he had drunk the whole glass of water. Hormozan then lifted the glass of water that had been provided to his lips, took one swallow, and then let the glass slip from his hands to the ground where it broke and the remaining contents spilled on the ground. The caliph then insisted the Hormozan had done this on purpose as a trick to avoid being killed and that he indeed must lose his life anyway.

But the people observing this tribunal insisted that Caliph Omar, successor to the honorable Mohammed, must keep his promise, saying in chorus, "The poor man did not finish drinking his glass of water. So you, as a person of divine provenance, must maintain your integrity and keep your promise not to kill him!"

When Hormozan sensed that now was his opportunity to save his life, he then settled the delicate issue and stated, "Right now, I accept Islam!" Indeed, the dispute was ended, and his life was spared.

Our story continues. Later on, Caliph Omar was assassinated by an Iranian. Obaido Allah, the son of Omar, suspected that Hormozan was responsible for his death. Eventually, this suspicion led Obaido Allah to kill Hormozan. Ottoman took the place of Omar and became caliph, the third successor after Mohammed and the first to follow Omar. He was advised by Imam Ali, son-in-law of Mohammed, that Obaido Allah had no right to kill Hormozan without a court hearing and that this action was entirely unjustified; he further reminded Ottoman that Obaido Allah deserved to be killed according to Islamic law. But Ottoman was hesitant to do such a deed for he reminded Imam Ali that the people already were mourning the death of Omar, Obaido

Allah's father, and that they would not be able to tolerate bringing Obaido Allah to court for killing Hormozan who, after all, was a non-Arab man and, in that sense, was "unworthy." This matter of discrimination rather than abiding by Islamic law was disturbing to Imam Ali, who further insisted that Hormozan was indeed Muslim and had been unjustly murdered by Obaido Allah, whom he swore to kill. Eventually, Imam Ali did kill Obaido Allah in the war of Siffin, and this revenge pleased Iranians; so is one of the reasons that they respect Imam Ali, a Shiite, as the first Imam even though he was believed by the Sunnis to be the fourth successor of Mohammed.

A final incident is important in establishing the important influence of Iran on Islam. When Islam became victorious in Persia during the reign of Omar, second successor of Mohammed, the princess Shahrbānū—daughter of the Persian king Yazdegerd who had been made a captive of the Arab Muslims—was rumored to have cursed Omar. Omar ordered that her head be shaved for this offense and that she be paraded through the streets of the city on a horse with her feet bound in chains, thus allowing all to see the beautiful princess in this humiliating stance. When Imam Ali heard about this order, he immediately countermanded the order by saying, "Do not do that! She did not curse you, Omar. But rather, she cursed her own ancestors for allowing the circumstances of Persia's defeat to take place. So she does not deserve such punishment and humiliation to occur." Omar relented and did not carry out his order. Furthermore, Imam Ali later arranged for the marriage of the princess to his son Husayn, who was the third Imam of the twelve Imams. Their son, offspring of an Iranian mother and an Arabian father (who was the great-grandson of Mohammed) thus became the fourth Imam, namely, al-Sajjad. His first name is Ali Zayn al-Abidin (worshiper's ornament)— Islam is divided in to three sects : Vahabi , Sunni, and Shiite. Pure Islam withouth any   alteration or vitiation is Vahaabi. The members of this sect base their faith only upon the literal translation of Koran; and they accept no directives from the so-called leaders or followers of Mohammed (the first four caliphs that were his successors), namely, Abū Bakr (first), Omar (second), Ottoman (third), and Ali (fourth).

These first four successors were either family members or associates of Mohammed, and they might be ranked as disciples. To my knowledge, Vahaabi are found only in Saudi Arabia. Among them are al Qaeda, whose leader is Osama bin Laden, who is from the Wohabi region. Those from that region oppose the Sunnis and the Shiites. Their doctrinal adherence is extreme.

Opposite to Vahaabi are the Sunnis, who follow both the Koran and the directives of the first four successors of the prophet Mohammed. These first four caliphs (Abū Bakr, Omar, Ottoman, and Ali) provide the substance of the belief of the Orthodox Sunni, and their teachings and commands delivered during their lives (or reign) have become the law for the Sunnis. There are four main branches of the Sunni: Hanafi (Iran and Egypt), Hanbali, Maliki, and Shāfi'ī. These four branches are named for leaders of different eras and provide the permanent substance of the jurisprudence of the Sunnis.

The Shiites accept the Koran; but they do not accept the directives of the first three caliphs or successors of Mohammed (Abū Bakr, Omar, and Ottoman), but only those teachings and commands of Ali, the fourth caliph in succession of Mohammed. In fact, they mostly disparage and even curse what the first three caliphs said and did. In addition to praising and accepting Ali, the Shiites also laud and honor his eleven sons as rightful successors of Mohammed; they are known as twelve Imams, or religious leaders, by this branch of Islam. There are three different groups of Shiites. The first branch is known as Zaidi, and they subscribe to the teachings and writings of the first four of the twelve Imams. Most of the Zaidi are living in Yemen along the Persian Gulf.

The second branch, or Ismāīlī, follow the directives of the first six of the twelve Imams. They live primarily in certain countries or areas that have a large Arab or Muslim population such as Pakistan, India, and Africa. Their present leader, originally an Iranian, worked for many years in the United Nations as the chief of refugee work. His honored title and name is Prince Agha Khan Mohalatti. Every twenty years, the Shiite leaders who follow the six Imams have contributed pure gold to charitable work that is the equivalent of the weight of their leader.

The third and the largest body of the Shiites, those Muslims who live mostly in Iran, believe and follow the teachings of all of the twelve Imams—starting naturally with the first Imam, who, again, was Imam Ali, the fourth caliph and son-in-law of Mohammed.

It now would be appropriate to explain a little more of the differences between Shiites and Sunnis, particularly as it might contribute to a better understanding of the situation in Iraq. Mahmud al-Aghad, an Egyptian who was a U.S. citizen and who was killed in Jordan as a Muslim Sunni, was a specialist in the faith of Islam. He wrote many books in Arabic language and in the English language too. In his book *Al-Abkareyat-Al Imam*, the prophet Mohammed had really commanded Ali, his uncle's son and his son-in-law, to be his successor; but he did not announce it or have it written as an order. Rather, he stated, "Whomever the majority of my companions and associates choose to be my successor will assume the leadership of my government at the time of my death." When that event occurred, those who were Mohammed's survivors and companions chose Abū Bakr, his father-in-law, to assume his leadership. They especially did not select Ali for several reasons, most particularly because of his relative youth and the fact that he had been the reputed instigator of the killings of a goodly number of his family. These survivors and associates of Mohammed held a deep resentment of Ali and wished to revenge these deaths but were helpless to subdue Ali because he claimed that he instigated these murders for the sake of Islam and not because of his own wishes.

The author also added that Omar said that the Koreish tribe decided that the government should not be led by Hashim because leadership should be shared with other tribes also and that Islam favors a practice in which, unlike other imperial forms of government, the leadership is not characterized by nepotism, with rule passed from one king only to his offspring. However, one Iranian specialist in Islam, a Shiite whose name is Sheik Abdul Hossein Amini, wrote a twenty-volume book entitled *Al Ghadir*, which was in response to writers like al-Ekad. All documentation in this book is based upon Sunni belief and states that according to Sunni Muslim writing, Ali was the real and first successor of Mohammed, but his right to leadership was usurped. Ali did not fight this decision because he wanted to avoid dissension that might weaken the young faith or even destroy it altogether. The government of Saudi Arabia did not allow this twenty-volume tome to be distributed in their country, and customs denied permission for it to be brought across the border. Thus, it has never been possible for the disputes between Shiites and Sunnis to be resolved! I met him personally when I was in Najaf, Iraq. He was there as an Iranian scholar and researcher with high regard.

Returning briefly to my Professor Fits, it is fair to say that it was his opinion, contrary to my statement that Islam is a religion for all the world, that Mohammed clearly felt that Islam is a blessing only for the people of the Arabian Peninsula. That is one reason that Mohammed did not recommend a successor for his close followers. The expansion of the faith has been due to the policies espoused by Abū Bakr, Omar, and Ottoman—the first three caliphs chose as successors to the Prophet. These policies called for the use of force to establish the growth of Islam, exactly as Mohammed had done on the Arabian Peninsula.

Abū Bakr had become the first successors to Mohammed by being the favorite of a majority of the Prophet's associates and companions. The success of Omar as the person to replace Abū Bakr as the second caliph at the time of his death was not determined in such a democratic manner for it was Abū Bakr who said (demanded) that Omar be the one to follow him as leader of the Muslim government, and when Omar was eventually murdered by unhappy subjects from Iran, he had already appointed six possible candidates as his successor (not including Ali) and had indicated that whoever received the majority approval by six consultants that he had appointed himself would be his successor. Omar had also declared that if there were a tie between these six candidates; then his son, Obaido Allah, would declare the winner. That somewhat limited process eventually resulted in the appointment of Ottoman as the third successor to Mohammed.

During the reign of Ottoman, conditions became very regimented, and he and his family enjoyed unusual privilege. Omar added that if any of the minority didn't accept the majority vote, they would be killed. As Islam was forced upon many outlying areas due to the military conquests of Ottoman and his family, particularly through the Persian Empire, Ottoman codified the Koran and brought it into writing according to his interpretation and in memory of Koran verses. It was his belief that Islam required one unified book of instructions for all believers to follow, and it had never been collected into book form. After thirty year death of Mohammed prophet Codi. Some Muslims who had committed the Koran to memory, such as Abd Allah ibn Mas'ud, disputed the correctness of Ottoman's version and, therefore, were exiled. The harshness of Ottoman is reflected in his reaction to this situation for he responded to the objections of Abd Allah ibn Mas'ud in extremely harsh language; ibn Mas'ud, in turn, reminded Ottoman that he had been a companion of Mohammed during a very trying time during the war of Ohud. Abd Allah found support from Aisha, Mohammed's widow, who happened to be present during this encounter. She informed Ottoman that Abd Allah was correct and that he was a very honorable man. Ottoman attempted to silence Aisha and told one of his strongmen servants to seize Abd Allah ibn Mas'ud and take him out of the mosque where they were meeting. The servant hoisted him over his shoulder, exited, and threw him to the ground so hard that many of Mas'ud's ribs were broken—an occurrence that eventually caused his death. Although Mas'ud's salary was then revoked by Ottoman, the many supporters of this unfortunate opponent of Ottoman provided financial assistance to him and his family. Sensing his impending death, Abd Allah ibn Mas'ud wrote in his will that Ottoman should not be permitted to attend his funeral and offer any prayers in his behalf.

At the time of Mohammed's death, Ali was thirty years old. As previously mentioned, Ali was very much in Mohammed's favor and certainly was a possible candidate to become his first successor; but according to the process that Mohammed had established for his successor to be chosen, he eventually lost to Abū Bakr, who became governor of Mecca following Mohammed's death. Ali cooperated with Abū Bakr during the time of his administration and happily accepted his rule. Abū Bakr appointed Omar to be his replacement as governor, and at the time of Abū Bakr's death, that succession was dutifully carried out. Ali accepted this course of events and endorsed Omar's authority, swearing his allegiance to this second successor to the Prophet. As a result of Omar's planning for his replacement, Ottoman was selected by an elite number of the hierarchical council. Again, Ali endorsed and cooperated with this third successor (caliph) of prophet Mohammed. The singular question as to why the Shiites do not accept these first three caliphs, even as their first Imam Ali did during their actual lifetimes, remains to be answered. As the English proverb suggests, perhaps all Shiites are "more Catholic than the pope." For some unclear historical enigma, the Shiites regard these first three caliphs as imposters who usurped the expected rights and reign of the fourth successor, Imam Ali! The Shiites remain adamantly critical of these three real-time ruling figures, even to the extent of actually cursing Omar, the second successor of the Prophet and the one whose miraculous role in history was actually to bring Persia to its knees and to convert it to the Muslim faith.

There is a point that some historians and scholars have forgotten when they fail to understand and wonder about the attitude of Shiites toward Abū Bakr, Omar, and Ottoman. All of these three caliphs considered themselves kings instead of governors, and they reflected a strong Arabic pride, exhibiting extremely prejudiced attitudes toward non-Arabic subjects. They discriminated against all who were not of Arabic lineage. And when it came to crediting forces other than Arabic for military victories that they accomplished, they gave no place to the role of Islamic faith nor even to Allah. Since the Shiites derive largely from Iranian background, most of them were very proud of the heritage of the Persian Empire and intuitively could cede little respect because of their feeling of superiority to Bedouins or any "uncivilized" group who might boast of victories that were really due to influential events and happenstances quite outside of their true power or control. And after all, it must be emphasized once again that the only reason, at least in the minds or Iranians, that the Islamic Arabians defeated the superpower Iranian armies was because of their reluctance to put up any sustained resistance in behalf of the Sassanid dynasty and their intense tyranny and oppression of their own ranks and of all Iranian citizens.

Indeed, it was only after allowing themselves to bow to the Islamic Arabian forces that Iranians began to realize that they had actually forfeited one tyrannical rule for another (from the outside) that was much worse and oppressive than their own native dynasty had been. Only after they began to experience the flagitious treatment that they incurred at the hands of their Arabic ruler did they comprehend the error of their ways. Indeed, the new life and society that they had settled for did nothing to change their destiny or improve their lot and, as stated, was even worse than that which they had experienced under the Sassanids. And what a bitter pill to swallow when Caliph Omar ordered the burning of all scholastic records and books, an action that prompted many Iranians to flee into exile in other countries. Finally, when tolerance was stretched to the breaking point, an Iranian assassinated Omar. Thus, it is that when one Iranian speaks in commination of another; traditionally, the person who is being reviled is likened to Omar, the accursed one. And so it is that Shiites, largely Iranian in background, have denied recognition or favor to Omar and to his predecessor and to the one who followed in his footsteps.

In summary, my point is that Islam was imposed upon Iran in such a way that the bad taste lingers in our memory and that those who are associated with this imposition have been excluded as effectively as possible from the spiritual side of the faith that transformed our society at that point in history. The additional emphasis that I wish to make is that there is a historic parallel in the event of 1979 when the rule of Khomeini was also imposed upon us, once again destroying the soul of a nation.

We must now consider how Ali eventually became caliph. Abū Bakr and Omar had a combined reign of about seventeen years, and Ottoman ruled for thirteen years. Following the completion of the rule of Ottoman, Ali was about sixty years old. As previously explained, during the control by Ottoman, there was extreme nepotism; and all of the political offices were occupied by family members. This circumstance was extremely upsetting to Muslims, and rebellion and resistance were continuously fomented. Ottoman was repeatedly under civil pressure to step down from his authority. At one point, Ali was able to achieve some conciliation between Ottoman and his subjects; but eventually, Ottoman failed to keep his promise. Soon, the people became rebellious again. There was a great gathering of revolutionaries about the palace of Ottoman one day; and finally, one bodyguard of Ottoman, one Kasur Ebne Shri Kennedy, shot into the crowd who were chanting for Ottoman to resign. The spokesman for the gathering who had shouted that Ottoman must step down was killed by the stray bullet.

The result was pandemonium, and the surging multitude wailed that Ottoman must release the bodyguard guilty of the crime to them. Ottoman's natural response was to reply that it was impossible for him to turn over one who was his supporter when his fate would be to be destroyed by those who wished to depose him. In short, his reply was that it was impossible to carry out their wish. Recognizing the impossibility of exacting revenge upon the usually obstinate Ottoman, the multitude completely surrounded the palace. Several of them climbed the forbidding walls and were actually able to enter a weakness of the fortification, intrude into the palatial confines, and kill Ottoman. This sudden, unexpected event left the Muslim government suddenly without any leadership, a situation that prevailed for five days.

Now Ottoman had always been very suspicious that Ali was behind the uprising. One of Ottoman's advisors had even counseled Ottoman to destroy Ali if he wanted to achieve peace for otherwise, it seemed that there would be an end to the rule of Ottoman. Although Ottoman had feared Ali too much because of his popularity to have him killed, still, he exiled him from Medina. Even though Ali had left the city as Ottoman had ordered, the uprising had only worsened in the absence of the much-respected Ali; and with the sudden turn of events, Ottoman had had no time to arrange for his successor. Certainly, if he had been in a favorable position, he would never have appointed Ali to be his successor, and there were two individuals who felt that they stood in line for that position. These two people were Talha and Zubair. Each was related to Ottoman, hence also to Ali. In particular, Zubair was also the son of an aunt of Mohammed's. Each of these individuals had been very close associates of Ottoman and had had a part in his appointment as caliph. They both had enjoyed positions of great favor, owning much property and wealth and living in much the same style as Ottoman. Possibly because of these great similarities to the slain leader, the revolutionary council entrusted with selecting a successor had little interest in approaching either Talha or Zubair for the leadership. Finally, all turned to Ali, whose election excited and pleased the entire host of revolutionaries who gladly, except for Talha and Zubair, confirmed the decision and swore allegiance to the designated choice. The rejected pair finally were forced to affirm their loyalty to Ali although they declared that they did so only out of fear for consequences of resisting the popular will and protested that they agreed only with drawn swords and a demand for a continuation for their positions of special favoritism.

As previously indicated, Ottoman was slain by people for revolution whose identities were unknown. As time progressed into the rule of Ali, Talha and Zubair soon defected from his leadership, largely because he had refused to grant their wishes for special privileges and, specifically, for their desire to become the governors of Basra and of Kufa, city-states of great prominence. They proceeded to promote an uprising against Ali and claimed that he was personally responsible for Ottoman's death, which they rightfully needed to revenge. They went so far as to contact Aisha, the surviving widow of the Prophet (and also the daughter of Abū Bakr), in order to seek her help in carrying their scheme of revenge against Ali. She assisted their cause by riding on a camel (the first war against Ali was known as Jamal, the camel) and carrying a bloody shirt of Ottoman's to arouse the sentiment of the people against Ali and his supposed part in the death of the third caliph. To this day, there is an Arabic saying that if you want to provide an excuse for something that did not really happen, you make an "Ottoman shirt," signifying that you are really not telling the truth.

To emphasize his concern for equality, Ali announced his plans to expand justice shortly after assuming authority. No one was to use government funds for personal gain, and all misused rewards that had been dispensed through governmental financing were to be returned to the source. He even refused to grant additional salary to his brother, Akiel, who had requested it because of his many children that he had to support. Ali's comment upon this matter was that his decision was based upon the fact that there were so many people much poorer than Akiel that such an injustice could not be countenanced. People of communistic persuasion in

Islam are the so-called mujahedeen Kalgh who borrowed Ali's reasoning as the basis for some of their principle teachings. They also suggested that one person's wealth is accumulated at the expense of others' deprivation and that all have equal rights before the law. There would be no poor or hungry unless someone else had trampled upon that which they deserved. Although such ideas became acceptable under Ali, they were exceptionally difficult to swallow by those who had been among the followers of Ottoman and further stiffened their reluctance to accept the new leader.

Thirty years before the death of Mohammed, the government of Islam came back again to Hashim from Umayya, a circumstance which, as previously mentioned, was very difficult for the Umayyads to accept because Hashim came into authority by forceful coercion of the Prophet.

The Koran pointed out that in every place you find a kafir, there are two meanings. One is that anyone who is not of the Muslim faith and challenges them must be killed. The other meaning of kafir is anyone, even a member of the Muslim faith, who speaks against Islam must be punished or even killed for being a blasphemer. For example, if one mullah (or priest) were to go to a village and an alderman (representative of the town) were not to provide him with proper respect and needed provisions immediately, the mullah had the authority to excommunicate him and to order him to be slain. This was exactly like Khomeini who, just at a whim, ordered so many intellectuals in Iran (even though they were exactly like him, both Muslim and Shiite) to be excommunicated and then, even without any court hearing, murdered.

A further example of the treatment of a kafir was when Omar appointed six individuals as counselors to determine his successor. If anyone opposed the decision of these counsels, they were ordered to be killed as kafirs immediately.

During the reign of Ali, Islam experienced three wars. All three of these conflicts pitted Muslim against Muslim. The first altercation, already briefly commented upon, was the war known as Camel. The second struggle was called Siffin and was a conflict between Ali and Muawiyah. In the confrontation, Muawiyah tricked Ali; and as a result, some of his own soldiers separated from his other forces and claimed that Ali was kafir because he accepted arbitration to settle the final outcome of the struggle. The people of Syria, under the command of Muawiyah, were very close to being defeated when they decided upon a strategy of trickery. They decided to mount the Koran on a high pole, effecting the symbolic meaning that they were followers of the holy writ. This devious action caused the armies of Ali to fall into disagreement, some claiming that since their opponents were fighting for the Koran just like they were, the struggle should be aborted. This faction was known as Khawārij. Even though Ali discerned the craftiness of his foe, his compatriots forced him into arbitration with Muawiyah, whose arbitrator (Amr b al-Aas) was a very clever and shrewd individual. Ali's representative at the bargaining table was a much older and less sophisticated person (Abu Musa Ashari). The debate at the intermediation came to a draw, and nothing was accomplished—a situation that resulted in rescuing Muawiyah from defeat, but one that caused nothing but trouble for Ali and eventually caused his demise.

Ali always asserted that it was not his wish to terminate the second of his wars by arbitration and that it was the insistence of the Khawārij that led to that eventuality. In fact, Ali fought his third conflict against the dissident Khawārij and defeated them. The survivors of these opponents of Ali plotted to kill Ali, Muawiyah, and Amr b al-Aas but, in the end, were only successful in the murder of Ali. Following Ali's death, his son Imam Hasan was unable to fight with Muawiyah and finally arrived at terms of conciliation: Iraq remained under the authority of Imam Hasan while Syria and some other territories remained under the governance of Muawiyah. Thus, the Koreish tribal leadership returned to the Banu Umayyads once again. Lots of confusion and intrigue—hardly what one of a truly divine and reverent intellect would imagine as providing a firm basis for reverent searching and belief.

In summary, as a result of the ascendancy of Mohammed, there was indeed a change in the social outlook of the people of the Arabian Peninsula. Prior to the life and teaching of the Prophet, the people of the peninsula lived as barbaric, nomadic Bedouins, always struggling with one another and without any controlling authority. Furthermore, before Mohammed, women commanded little respect, female babies were a shame for a father, and families even sacrificed them by burying them alive; and there were probably only five literate persons living on the entire peninsula. Changes for the better in each of these societal circumstances were the blessing of Allah achieved through the reforming effect of the life and actions of the Prophet!

And let me emphasize again that the prevailing circumstances that allowed Mohammed to have this transforming effect upon the society and politics of his native land were the facts that he belonged to the tribe of Koreish, widely respected leaders for years in that territory, and that Khadijah was wealthy, which the business savvy of the Prophet allowed him to use skillfully to the utmost advantage. Other factors that permitted Mohammed to prevail were the "fear of the sword of Ali," Mohammed's cousin and son-in-law, and the eventual fourth caliph but first Imam of the Shiites. No small influences in the achievement of dominance by the Prophet was his determination in terms of forceful persuasion ("Accept Islam, or your neck will be cut") and the unfailing allegiance of his followers to extend the influence of Mohammed. When Mohammed's cohort fought the enemy, should they have been killed in the process, they were promised entry into heaven immediately with rewards of an Arcadian kingdom and delights beyond imagination; or should they have survived, there always was great booty to divide among the hardy battlers.

Finally, the three successful wars waged by Mohammed extended his dominance just as rain might refresh a dry garden. His opponents—Ohud, Badr, and Khaibar—were formidable persons in their own right, and their defeat by the forces of the Prophet brought great reward for the founder of Islam.

After Mohammed's death, these three immediate successors expanded, by means of war, the influence of the faith throughout the Persian Empire, Egypt, and Syria; but unlike the effects of the Prophet's conquests during his lifetime upon the society of the peninsula, as already emphasized previously, the benefits to mankind of the further spread of the faith were negligible. On the contrary, the ensuing growth of Islam in extent of its domain had negative effects upon the destinies of its victims—particularly in the areas of education, intellectual pursuits, and civil freedom. Furthermore, many innocent lives were destroyed as the Islamic hordes attempted to impose their ideals upon an unwilling force of infidels—any Islamic government, either past or present, that provides true justice, prosperity, freedom, peace, or a life of ease for its subjects.

In conclusion, the following problems and their solutions are uncovered. In the current struggle between the Western powers and the Middle Eastern countries, a conflict that the West justifies "in the name of freedom," Palestine, al Qaeda, and other Islamic factions justify their opposition as kafir *harbi* in nature (the proper alliance against those who are non-Muslim). Much has been written about this struggle. Quite naturally, each analysis is interpreted from the point of view of the author; but unfortunately, little attention has been provided to identify the root cause of the contention. To reach a solution without understanding the basic reason for the existing dilemma is an impossibility, just as it would be unlikely that a physician would be able to treat an illness without identifying the underlying disorder. But before we do proceed to discuss the actual root cause of the current turmoil, let me reemphasize two more points.

First, let me again call attention to the fact that the West has used its intelligence and creativity in such a manner as to become superior by virtue of establishing predominance in education, social capability, scientific technology, military prowess, and political organization. So for many years, they have colonized and subjugated weaker nations in order to capitalize upon their resources for their own benefit and have actually plundered the wealth of these less formidable countries. This pattern of ill-treatment became sort of an addition of the West. And then when Churchill discovered the primacy of oil in the international struggle for wealth and power, all efforts, whether overt or covert, were directed toward achieving access to this all-important commodity. In short, the greater the efforts of a nation for surpassing others in all aspects of progress, the greater the requirement for oil. Acquisition of this important resource became either the basic drive for colonization or the very reason not to colonize but rather to subjugate. What use for diplomacy if by might and power one could finesse or seize the oil and have to govern it as well nor worry about the rights of native citizens?

A point that I have implied and stated outright time and time again: the beginning of difficulty for Middle Eastern countries is their resource of oil. And this is especially true for Iran. I know and can unequivocally state that all the entanglements in this region of our world have been for the sake of oil. All the embraces and salutes trace their motivation to the intrigues deriving from the desire for acquisition of that number one commodity—oil! And when bad feelings supervene, the slander and curses emanate from the failure to secure this black gold. The slaughter of the masses and the maiming of the military stem from the burning urges to acquire this main item of capital and industry. Lies and deception are the currency exchanged for the control of this commodity, and all inhumanities to man is based upon the amassing of large stores of this liquid energy source. Each coup d'etat had its fomentation and growth wrapped in the interstices of the fight to control this basic material. The very establishment of the nation of Israel in the territory of Palestine by the West was because of the oil of the Middle East. The 1979 reimposition of Islam upon the nation of Iran was based ultimately upon the wish to control the ebb and flow of this substance.

There have been a number of historical happenings with the background motivational force related to the accomplishment of handy access to oil resources. A number of small governments have been established around the Persian Gulf with their basic reason for existence relative to interests in the acquisition of oil by several of the global powers. As already alluded to, an underlying cause for the ongoing struggle between Israel and the Arabs depends upon the desire of the West to keep closer scrutiny upon the disposition of oil resources. And again, the toppling of the shah of

Iran, with its dire consequences to that nation, was a joint effort upon the part of England, France, and the USA entirely for the sake of controlling the management of oil resources.

This coup d'etat was accomplished by international subterfuge and was later followed up by the application of sanctions by the United States, an affront carried out for the sake of oil. And finally, the present embargo against electricity being produced in Iran from atomic sources as well as uranium enrichment for any purpose is all for the sake of oil.

Another interesting thing: The United states o f America has full sanctions against any trade with Iran, with the exception of one commodity; namely, the sale of cigarettes or tobacco. Because these items contain nicotine and are known as provokers of cancer, there is no sanction against their sale to Iran. Since they do not enhance health or the economy of a people, no embargo is placed upon the sale of these items to my country, and Iran is the third largest importer of cigarettes from the USA in the world.

In summation then, Iran and its people suffer oppression and torture primarily because of oil. Secondly, the geographic situation of the country of Iran next to the Strait of Hormuz, through which pass nearly more than twenty five percent of the world's oil, leaves them in the unhappy circumstance of being the object of persecution and degradation. And since Iran is the mother country of this region of the world and has a proud history of world dominance at one stage in the story of civilization, it now bears the brunt of the debasement and arrogance of its global peers. Its unique situation as a basic partner to the language and ethnic origins of so many leaves it as a brother to many peoples, and just as the brothers of biblical Joseph placed him in the well and sold him into slavery because of filial jealousy, so also now the world returns its envious wrath upon Iran and has immersed it in a well of fire to burn hopelessly. Thus, there is little compassion for an underdog nation whose citizens are whipped, stoned, and torn limb from limb; and there is no concern for a hapless generation whose women are abused, whose population has no employment, and who suffer the irony of wealth without money!

The Iranian imperial regime initiated policies designed to bring Iran to the same level of economic and technological capability as European countries. Its general approach was based upon the national interests of its own country and upon creating friendly relations with all nations in the world. The government instigated many petrochemical projects and stimulated research in increasing the uses of petroleum. They encouraged investment in any processes that might lead to new petroleum products. Under his Emperor Mohammed Reza Shah's guidance, Iran became one of the nine wealthiest global entities. The growing industrialization and scientific emphasis proved to be a threat to the major Western powers, so they used the traditional interest in religion as a tool to entice the overthrow of this progressive leader and to impose a regressive religious dictatorship in 1979. As has been implied and asserted on multiple occasions already, present-day Iran is suffering indescribably under the authority of this repressive theocracy.

As many of us are aware, it was conspiracy among big oil companies that has destroyed the country of Iraq. It is apparent now that Iraq had no connections with al Qaeda nor did it have weapons of mass destruction. Iraq could never have been any threat to the West at all. It is quite likely that the lobbyists in Washington for the nation of Israel came to the realization that

Iraq's oil reserves might threaten the future of their country. When they considered that both the vice president and president of the most powerful nation in the world had major personal interests in the oil industry, then they inferred that the situation of Iraq's huge oil reserves would not and could not be ignored and that any circumstance suggesting the takeover of the Middle East by Iraq would be intolerable. Whereas before the preemptory attack upon Iraq by the United States, it was estimated that Iraq had a reserve of one hundred billion barrels of oil. It is now widely accepted that Iraq in fact has over 216 billion barrels of reserve oil.

With so much misinformation and misunderstanding surrounding such an immense undertaking, it is extremely troubling to consider that over two hundred million individuals whose lives have been immersed in turmoil have been forced to evacuate their Iraqi homeland and that each day, sectarian violence now continues to cost the lives of close to one hundred of the remaining civilians, innocent women and children among them. Add to this the destruction turned loose on the lives of U.S. military families with the loss of young men and women in their lives' prime and the maiming of many more, both physically and psychologically, through the indiscriminate and explosive destruction that is continually occurring on a daily basis. Consider also that over a trillion dollars have been invested in this struggle, not to mention the billions more that will be expended on Iraqi relief and reconstruction, including both physical and psychological reconstitution. Out of all this, will it be possible to achieve a satisfying oil strategy for the West or permanent peace for Israel? In other words, can there be an outcome of this imbroglio that will actually provide a positive change as well as both national and international security? This question haunts all intellectuals here and abroad.

Such a group of highly minded intellects known as the Oxford Research Group (ORG), founded back in 1982 in London, continue today as a seriously motivated body of nongovernmentals—that is, studying such issues as the impact of this present war (which we have now labeled as a war against terrorism) upon global security. Could there not be an alternative course in the achievement of a calm and peace among human beings?

In the outset of this writing, it was stated that human beings are dependent upon one another for their very existence. In the terms of today's politics and social circumstances, this might be stated as, "The West needs Middle Eastern oil, and the Middle East stands in the profound dilemma of requiring Western technology and social implementation for survival." Is there no other way of satisfying this interrelatedness besides mutual self-destruction and the intolerable humiliation and degradation of body and soul?

As an example of this interrelatedness, were it not for technology of the United States in Saudi Arabia, the Bedouin camel rider in the hot desert would never have been able to search for the oil under the ground or in the sea to refine it and sell it throughout the world nor to develop over seventy thousand different products derived from petroleum. And so today, the poor camel rider (such as Osama bin Laden) and many others, due to the myriad blessings stemming from the oil industry, have become millionaires and billionaires who enjoy the latest modern conveniences and means of transport (beyond the humble camel). By means of their wealth accumulated from this huge industry, some of these magnates spawned from the financial pyramid created have used their means to take revenge upon the exploiters of their lands and are causing the death of Westerners and (now) Iraqis. Meantime, foreign politicos and the oil companies continue to collect humongous revenues as profits from the petroleum industry and, in turn, foment unrest and intrigue in order to keep the Middle East in a steady state of intimidation and instability, not caring in the least for the resultant death and maiming of their own military conscripts and humanitarian workers. And as long as these conditions are allowed to prevail, inhumane events and insecurity on both sides of the issue will continue to evolve. The selfish and uncompassionate policies *must be terminated*! Rather, programs of love, understanding, honesty, and justice must replace the double-dealing and deception that now grip this planet. Only then shall all mankind benefit from the right use of God's creation!

The tragedy of the war proceeding from the horrific events of 9/11 was based on the pretext of a struggle against terrorism. It commenced in Afghanistan and next was fashioned into a war to eliminate Saddam Hussein and to liberate the people of Iraq. Saddam was alleged to have weapons of mass destruction and was threatening the Middle East with a takeover by his armies. The question I pose is, "What was the real cause for the dastardly attack of 9/11 upon the United States?" (Politicians use Sophistry in their response and supply only a symptom for the question.)

Osama bin Laden, acting as a Muslim Vahaabi, and some Muslim Sunnis, acting as the Taliban, established al Qaeda as a radical Mohammedan coterie. In Iran, some Shiites established Hezbollah. These radical Muslim groups killed many innocent fellow Muslims in the name of Allah. These organizations and their actions were symptomatic of a much deeper problem that urged them into the pursuit of their activities. Not mentioned were the real fomenters of what was taking place. Unmentioned are the names of Jimmy Carter, former president of the United States; James Callaghan, the prime minister of Great Britain; nor Valéry Giscard d'Estaing, the president of the French Republic.

But in fact, it was due to their actions under the pretext of fighting for human rights that these radical groups received the motivation to surge forward and to broaden their dastardly much more global activities. The fact indeed was that these fanatical organizations of Muslims were in a small minority, without any firm base or support nor money or any national undergirding but received the necessary prompting to secure these required backings that allowed them to become formidable enemies because of the deceptively "righteous" undertakings of the Western leaders just named.

Thus, when the Communist party in Afghanistan made their coup d'etat in 1978 in Afghanistan and asked the Soviet Union to send assistance by the Red Army, much to the surprise and shock of these Western political leaders, the afore-named heads of the Western powers, frightened by this unexpected turn of events (that would allow Russia to approach the Persian Gulf), suddenly altered their global strategies and decided to foster the radical Islamic extremists and back their ideology against that of the Afghan Communists and their military comrades from the North. This action by the West propelled the Islamic fanaticism in Afghanistan and, together with the overthrow of the shah in Iran through Western political subterfuge already discussed, abetted the rise of the Hezbollah in Iran. It also left two major countries in this region, Afghanistan and Iran, under the authority of Islamic fanatic regimes. It did keep Russia out of the Persian Gulf by the ejection of its army from Afghanistan, but eventually, it allowed for the plotting that led to the dastardly attack of 9/11 and the subjection of free peoples of these two nations to Islamic dictatorships. Easier access to oil was a temporary consequence in Iran, but as is now apparent, even that was only a short-term benefit to the West. Such access may have been a motivating force that led to the preemptive invasion of Iraq, but here too, that has proven to be a thorn rather than a blessing and may not have promoted the security of Israel.

In summary, this strategic policy of the West allowed a minor religious fanaticism to rise to prevalence and bring destruction and desolation to the people of Iran. It was promoted, as already indicated, to preserve human rights but has led to circumstances in Iran that never before were endured by its people, including public castigation of the innocent, the severing of hands as punishment, and the actual performance of stoning as retaliatory consequence for allegation of unproven misbehavior. At present, only a handful of Iran's political leadership benefit from the profits of oil production, and there is an unemployment rate of 80 percent throughout the country. The general population of Iran is downcast, and the country is one thousand years behind the rest of the world socially and thirty years in arrears technologically as well.

In review then, whenever one listens to the media and a representative of the Western governing authority speaks about Islamic terrorists or of Osama bin Laden or of the Taliban or of Hezbollah, the blame for awful and frightening events and atrocities occurring in the world today is laid at their feet and properly so. But no one ever engages in a critical analysis that goes back behind these happenings and mentions the role of any of the Western political leaders already discussed whose policies actually led to the creation of these terroristic proponents or to the steps that brought them into the positions of prominence that they have assumed today. My concern in this is that citizens of the West are misled and thus fail to acknowledge the mistaken strategies that have eventuated in the unsavory conditions that now prevail in Iran, Iraq, Afghanistan, Palestine, Lebanon, and elsewhere. Failing to recognize our own guilt and our role in the developments of the situations that now prevail will only blind us when making the necessary changes in our global political strategies that must be made if we are to appropriately modify and correct the injustices that exist. And unfortunately, it indeed may be too late for necessary changes to be made.

Furthermore, there are interests in our sphere of the globe that would prefer that things do not change too radically in the rest of the world. If it could be made out to seem that many Middle Easterners are just not ready to accept democracy and the freedoms that we enjoy, then these interests feel more certain of their ability to protect their oil profits. Such will more likely not be challenged, and it is better to maintain the status quo than to deal compassionately with "poor" subjects not yet ready for the streamlined social and political graces that the West is trying to impose in the same old manner and atmosphere of might makes right (or the same old colonialism of the past). And this process begins with the appointment of a puppet who does not always carry out the directions of his superiors but tortures and violates those beneath him with the assumption that those in authority will support this mismanagement and the abuse of power. For after all, this is the way things have been for centuries, with people of the Middle Eastern region deprived of their freedom and of the advantages of modern living. Certainly, these subjects have the same feelings and expectations as those who would continue to hold them back, but they are powerless to express these wishes. In fact, their situation is much like those of Afro-American origin in the seventeenth, eighteenth, and nineteenth centuries in the United States, except the skins of the Middle Easterners are not quite as pigmented. But there is no need to recycle this unfortunate history of discrimination again; rather, compassion must replace ignorance, personal disregard, and aloofness.

Indeed, Western countries with their more advanced civilities and freedom must become like caring teachers offering service and help to the many who are disadvantaged and underdeveloped. Were this attitude to prevail in our global relations, respect and gratitude would be returned, and the world would become a peaceful and enjoyable Shangri-la for all to mutually live in and enjoy.

As a final summation, may I reiterate that the root of the problem has been that the Western nations have built their foreign political policies upon Sophism (lies and deception) and the philosophy of Protagoras and Thrasymachus in the belief that there is no basis for treating those who are in an inferior position with kindness or justice, that might is right (Plato), and that authority is exerted for the benefit of those holding sway. Ideals of personal responsibility have been lost, and Western politicians continue to turn their backs upon justice and equality in the way that they treat representatives of other cultures. And when called to an accounting for the adverse effect of what they have allowed to take place, they deny any personal responsibility for events but cite politics and consequences as the result of political maneuvering beyond their control, as if politics is an abstract entity that excuses personal accountability.

One of the most flagrant examples of which I have just spoken is the criticism of Jimmy Carter leveled at President Bush and Prime Minister Tony Blair concerning the current conflict that we are engaged in with terrorism, a conflict that has come about because of political strategies that he, President Carter, and then British prime minister James Callaghan took mutual part in back in the 1976–1980 period under the guise of working for "freedom and democracy" and which allowed the very terroristic entities to come into being (previously explained), with which we are currently doing battle. In short, the extremist factions achieved their current status of power and capability during the administrations of Carter and Callaghan when they instigated the destruction of Iran and the installation of an Islamic Shiite regime that puts all people of proud Persian heritage to shame as well as promoted the Taliban in Afghanistan that predated al Qaeda and eventually brought about the shameful catastrophe of 9/11. This does not lessen the magnitude of the present-day mistakes perpetuated by President Bush and British Prime Minister Blair in behalf of freedom and democracy, but the stance of Carter tends to turn into oblivion and erases his role and responsibility for what has come to pass and his errors that led to the current unfortunate circumstances.

In Farsi tradition, there is a proverb that states that "Goldsmith's guising fight" is the quality whereby an argument between two is intended to deceive a third party. Maybe Carter's criticism of Bush and Blair is a deceptive maneuver to exonerate him in our eyes for decisions that definitely were fallacious but notwithstanding later (2002) allowed him to receive a Nobel Peace Prize for his efforts in behalf of peace and justice throughout the world. As you may infer, as a displaced Iranian, I cannot be an unqualified admirer of former president Jimmy Carter because of the tragedy of Iran beyond the era of the shah; but in fairness, I do recognize good things that he has done after the global misdeeds of his administration as president of the United States! But maybe when he suggested that Blair's approval of Bush's war policy was "flattering," he was suggesting that had not the British prime minister praised Bush's policies in such a blanket manner, the U.S. president might not have been encouraged to go ahead with his preemptive attack upon Iraq. Indeed, Carter's insinuation was that Blair "cajoled" Bush into the struggle that we now have come to regret and for which we have paid such a high price in so many ways, not to mention the tragic effects that the nation of

Iraq has suffered. Indeed, the affable relationship between Great Britain and the United States is an admirable circumstance on the stage of international diplomacy, and Jimmy Carter is too much of a gentleman and person of political etiquette and rectitude to epitomize an action of one leader in regard to another as an instance of "wheedling." But the Sophistry that characterizes British international policy is both mysterious to understand and devious in its effects, and as already suggested, Carter himself was led into some unforgivable actions that involved the influence of the United Kingdom and resulted in the desolation of my nation and the promotion of terrorism in ways difficult to imagine at that time in history. Certainly, when any political decision is acted upon by the United Kingdom, there is a duplicitous effect that not only assures benefit to the imperial hierarchy, but also maintains the position of dependency on the part of the global region being dealt with—a very studied outcome.

I note also that when Prime Minister Blair retired recently from his position of leadership of Great Britain, he said, "I have done everything that I thought was good for the United Kingdom." He spoke truthfully for he did not say that he had done what was good for the world or for humanity or for justice in the world. British politicians act in behalf of their nation although they are not always so forthright in declaring that intention. I think that since the United States of America has been jettisoned into the situation where its citizens are stigmatized and are unsafe in any place in the world through the crafty support supplied by Mr. Blair for Mr. Bush and labeled flattery by Jimmy Carter, we should call a spade a spade and fairly admit that we have been downstaged by the cleverness of British "diplomacy" and try to figure out the best way to extricate ourselves from this global position of shame and insecurity.

Never before in world history has the reference to our president been so shabby as it is currently. So many world politicians—such as the Russian president, the president of Venezuela, and Iran's Ahmadinejad openly—insult George W. Bush and make offensive statements about him, his actions, and policies when they speak at international events or before the United Nations. When the president travels abroad, he confronts demonstrations and placards that carry adverse slogans and that represent a negative attitude from the populace of the countries in which he is visiting. There has been a drastic change in the reception that he used to receive before the undertaking of this preemptive struggle in Iraq.

It is also noticeable that European countries like England, France, and Italy are not under the pressure and influence of the Israel lobby, especially if they express no open opposition to actions of the government of Israel. Each European nation has its own strong determination; and when Blair acted against the will of his people by joining with the United States in its ill-advised venture in Iraq, neither France, Germany, nor Russia joined with the United Kingdom in this decision to support President Bush. We certainly must surmise that there may well have been some underlying motive not clearly discernible to the average person that resulted in Blair's action. By this deceptive support of Bush, Blair was able to take back Europe's position as a superpower in the world. The value of the dollar was lowered while that of the euro was elevated.

Jimmy Carter's employment of the term "flattering" reminds me of the last banquet he attended in Niavaran Palace, an occasion honoring Carter and sponsored by the shah. At that time, he used words of flattery in regard to the shah by stating that Iran under his authority was like an island of stability and peace in the Middle East. He also read the poem by the famous Iranian poet

Saadi to the effect that humans are like one body and that when one part suffers, the whole body suffers, further adding that if you are not concerned with the pain of others, you do not deserve to be called human. Carter emphasized the idea that the world did not have another example so fine as Iran, one with such an outstanding culture. Carter used this tactic of flattery to deceive the shah, and then he participated in the destruction of the nation of Iran. No wonder he termed a similar action of deception as "flattery," a tactic with which he was all too familiar.

By the skull drudgery of human rights utilized by Jimmy Carter, the mullah Khomeini was able to leash the Iranian nation to the yoke of Hezbollah, making of these once proud Persians their slaves and *akhfash* goat! And the title of superpower now applies not only to the United States, but also to Europe, Russia, and China, with India lurking in the background as a fifth such entitlement.

Chapter Seven

Conclusion and Solution

As I draw toward a conclusion, I note again from summarizing opinions drawn from different factual sources (media) that intellectuals who provide interpretations of history regard Western powers as more dominant because they refuse to put aside their own cultural standard that might is right; simply stated, they refuse to accept the cultural concepts of truth and justice as seen from the viewpoint of their opponents. On the other hand, proponents of Middle East philosophy (primarily followers of Islam or of Hebrew faith) adhere to a doctrine of revenge and destruction of their opposition. They also refuse to change their style and reject attitudes of love, equality, and compassion for justice for all. Thus, the two sides in this modern world's conflict find communication and exchange of reason extremely difficult, and grounds for a truce in their competition for supremacy is extremely difficult to achieve.

Of course, it is my contention that tyranny and killing of innocent people is never justified—whatever the circumstances, whether in the name of freedom or of Allah. In short, there is never "justification for injustice." I once heard that an intelligent group of Hebrews in London under the name of Independent Jewish Voices was attempting to establish communication between Jewish and Muslim followers in order to broach a solution between the two sides, the Palestinian and Israeli governments. Success in such a process is extremely tenuous in my opinion.

When I was a student of religion in Najaf, Iraq, during 1950, one of the Western committees sent a letter inviting an Arab Shiite Islamic leader in that city (Ayatollah al Kashef al-Ghetah) to a conference entitled "All Believers in God in Unity against Communists in the Soviet Union" that was to take place in Bahmedun, Lebanon. Kashef al-Ghetah declined the invitation and wrote a small book in Arabic, the title of which was *Mosolol-Olya-Fel-Islam*, meaning "The Virtues of Good Ethics in Islam." In the summary of his book, he wrote that he would not participate in a conference with Jews who are the occupiers of Palestine nor with Christians who are supporters of these occupiers. "The Communists of the Soviet Union did not occupy Arabic land nor did they kill nor wage war with Palestinian Arabs. They did help us in the past to fight against Israel and are helping us even now. In consideration of these circumstances, Islamic ethics will not allow us to join with an enemy of Palestine and Arabs to rally against a friend who is the enemy of our enemy. The virtues of good behavior is not in Bahmedun, but rather in Islam. What you, as believers in God, did in Palestine, not even the Communists who do not believe in God would do in any place in the world!"

In the United States, the government has seemed to become paralyzed due to the excessive influence of the Jewish lobby. The affected departments include the administration and the cabinet, both Democratic and Republican sides of Congress, and important governmental agencies—especially those dealing with the Middle Eastern affairs. The media is also heavily pressured by this lobby.

As an illustration of this overwhelming influence of the Jewish lobby, it is interesting to note that the majority of people in the United States now have become disenchanted with the war in Iraq. In order to express this opposition effectively, a large portion of the electorate swung their support away from the Republicans and voted for Democrats in the 2006 elections. The general sentiment, however, is that nothing really different will happen because both parties are so strongly subservient to manipulation by the Jewish lobby. As the old Persian axiom suggests, "The yellow dog is also brother of the jackal." It seems that the only option to express disfavor of presidential policies was to vote his opposition power into office, even though this prevailing sentiment of frustration exists that the Jewish lobby controls both sides and little change actually will take place, even with the rejection of the Republicans. As one individual expressed to me, "Even though I realize that no real change in Middle Eastern policy will take place with the change in majority rule, I voted for the Democrats just to express my dissatisfaction to the president and to let him know I am not happy with his attitudes and actions."

It is my personal opinion that the politicians of the United States are running for Congress and for the presidency somewhat out of the sense of tradition to do so in a democracy but that they have become so compliant to the sources of their biggest financial support that they do their legislating and decision making primarily for the continued backing of these sources. Since many of the biggest corporations in the United States are under the control of a Jewish constituency, their demands are insulated through their lobby, and relatively few candidates feel any freedom to exercise a truly financially unrestricted opinion in their approach to the issues before them.

I also sense that it was the decision of the president, under the influence of these Jewish and big business lobbies, to go to war in 2003 and that he felt that there were enough indications that could justify such an action that he might logically convince the voting constituency that there was distinct plausibility in committing such a preemptive action. It is also my intuition that a majority (80 percent) of this voting constituency are normally Christian and would not willingly approve of this biased influence were they truly aware of the extent of this power. Indeed, the largest segment of the voting population of the United States have a sincerely kind and compassionate attitude toward all peoples of the world, regardless of their race or creed—be they Hindu, Muslim, colored, or what have you. These U.S. citizens are basically believers in the ideals that truth, freedom, peace, love, and real justice must prevail. These principles are at the heart of their Christian faith, and any foreign policy based on the idea that might is right, regardless of the destruction that it brings to innocent people of any ilk, should not be tolerated. And as a further tenet of their beliefs, most U.S. citizens agree that any empowered group, whether through financial capability or religious bias, should not have the special privilege of exerting authority over the decisions of elected officials. In short, the havoc that we have wreaked in Iran and Iraq is basically quite unacceptable with the majority in the United States, and deception is not their approved approach to global matters.

It might be relevant to report at this point a conversation that I had with my friend and the translator of my writings from Farsi, Dr. Knauer and his wife, Mary. They had remarked about Jimmy Carter and his admirable participation in Habitat for Humanity since he was in retirement after his presidency. They had also praised him for his teaching over the years in Sunday school at the Baptist church in Americus, Georgia, that he attends. Both Dr. Knauer and his wife had celebrated their fiftieth anniversary by participating in a habitat build conducted by Carter and Millard Fuller, founder of Habitat, in Durban, South Africa (they were part of a group from the U.S. National Council of Churches led by then NCC chairman, the Reverend Robert Edgar). They had described the significant dedication of each of one hundred dwellings by the presentation of a Bible by Carter and Fuller (and their wives) to each recipient of a new home. This certainly was a meaningful event to have taken place, and I agreed with their praise of the ex-president.

Nonetheless, I interrupted their eulogy and underlined my concern that although Carter in recent years has done many things having great value in service to mankind, still, his preceding global policies with regard to Iran during his presidency had been responsible for the loss of homes and possessions of millions of Iranians and also in the loss of many innocent lives during the war between Iran and Iraq that resulted in fact due to these foreign policies carried out (for "human rights") during his administration of the United States between 1976 and 1980.

I then continued my criticism by pointing out that even the hostage crisis during his presidency in the United States was replete with lies and deception. Even though it is difficult for me to prove that which I am about to share—and there is a world of difference between the information that I will discuss and that which is recorded in our recollections and textbooks dealing with the events and time to which I am about to refer—I am confident that each scenario that I will discuss was, in fact, planned and executed with the design of forcing the Soviet Union to abandon its war effort and to evacuate its forces from Afghanistan. And if you should question my interpretation of these historic incidents, I may refer you to a text written in Farsi by a correspondent named

Azadeh who reported and recorded these very times and events for the Christian Science Monitor and for the Boston Club.

It is in chapter 15 of that Farsi document that the most important paragraphs that underlie the matters that I am about to report are and which I have translated into English from their written recording in Farsi.

Item 1: At the time that the Soviet Union occupied Afghanistan, it was a main concern of U.S. President Jimmy Carter to provide, in secret, munitions and articles of defense to the opponents of this occupation. In clandestine fashion, he and his collaborators were able to send these war materials through Pakistan and to supply the rebels and certain warlords (mujahedeen) actively combating the Russian troops.

Item 2: Such an effort was impossible in the western part of Afghanistan for there the Soviet forces were in complete control along with their Afghan Communist counterparts. In a large part of that rugged country, the weapons of the native forces opposing the Soviets were outmoded, and there was a paucity of appropriate ammunition. To attempt to send any help to the western section of Afghanistan, there was no other way of entry other than through Iran.

Item 3: Thus, the U.S. administration with President Carter's direction sought a pretext that would allow channeling of aid through Iran in order to assist the Afghan rebels and devised a plan that would mask this operation and provide feasibility to the procedure. With the advice of politically skilled strategists and after careful examination of all aspects of the issues involved, they came to the conclusion of creating the hostage situation, a strategy that would permit the assistance to Afghanistan and reap several other benefits:

1. As a friend of the United States, the shah had provided assistance to old friends like Gerald Ford, Richard Nixon, and Henry Kissinger. With a group of hostages being held by the new revolutionary regime in Iran, the shah would not be in a position to request these former allies to help him to go back to Iran and resume his leadership position as king of that country for were he to make such a request, our U.S. authorities would say that we cannot risk the lives of these fifty-three individuals being held captive in Tehran. "So sorry, there is no way that we can help you in this way under these conditions." And surely, the shah would not persist in such a petition for he would not wish to endanger the lives of these fifty-three captive U.S. citizens. Ironically, the shah could not even get permission to live in exile in the United States because of the hostage situation, and it was only through the mediation of Henry Kissinger that he was permitted to undergo surgery and follow-up therapy in New York; following which, it was declared too dangerous for him to remain in the United States, and he was forced to find asylum in Panama.

2. The new hijackers, the radicals, and anti-U.S. factions in Iran would rejoice because they would believe that the ultimate power of the United States in Iran had been shattered.

3. With the situation of hostages, the U.S. government could seize Iranian assets and investments and refuse to release them until the imprisonment was ended.

4. The entire population of the United States would be united in their antipathy toward Iran, and any action to

secure release of the hostages would be supported and applauded by U.S. citizens.

5. The general attitude of the world's politicians and leaders would turn against Iran, and dignity and honor of this ancient nation would be besmirched; Iran's dominance in the Middle East would suffer.

6. It would become quite easy to foment war between Iraq and Iran, the two largest exporters of oil in this region. Much of the Iranian reserves (218 billion dollars on that time) would logically be spent by Russia, Europe, and the United States on military items while Iraq, a country lacking the financial wealth of Iran, would receive monetary support from Saudi Arabia, Kuwait, and the United Arab Emirates since Arabs disdain Iranians and Iranians do not admire Arabs.

7. In the guise of attempting to rescue our hostages, we would be able to funnel ammunition and military supplies through Iran into western Afghanistan along its long border with the Iranian nation, thereby accomplishing the support that the West wished for the Afghan rebels (mujahedeen) in their struggle with the Soviet Union.

All of these strategic points are the major ones among many more reasons that the hostage crisis was believed to be a satisfactory plan to pursue by the Carter administration. To meet this perceived challenge, the Soviet Union installed highly technical radar surveillance along the western border of Afghanistan and placed many antimissile encasements close to Iran in the high mountains between the two countries. This move rendered the infusion of Western military supplies into Afghanistan a very unlikely maneuver.

Then on April 25, 1980, at 4:30 a.m., President Jimmy Carter was informed that an antiaircraft missile of the Soviet Union had

149

struck several U.S. helicopters and that eight U.S. airmen had been killed while at least four others were badly burned. After emergency consultation with advisors, it was decided that President Carter should call the general secretary of the Communist Party, Brezhnev, on the exigency phone set up between the two leaders for just such an occasion. After many words exchanged in anger and disagreement, President Carter insisted that these aircraft had been sent as part of a mission to rescue the hostages in Tehran. Brezhnev refuted that argument by insisting that such a situation as put forth by President Carter was impossible since the distance between Tabas (near where the helicopters were downed) and Tehran is 1,052 kilometers (about seven hundred miles) while the distance from Tabas to the western Afghanistan border is only about sixty miles.

Brezhnev further pointed out that the hostages were not in the U.S. Embassy building in Tehran but were widely known to be held in the Iranian foreign ministry building in Tehran. He added that the U.S. Embassy building in Tehran was surrounded by myriads of land mines, so it would not have been feasible to try to land there, much less with all the munitions that were on board the downed aircraft. Brezhnev then advised President Carter that if he told his U.S. citizens that Soviet missiles had downed the aircraft, he would justify this action by telling the world the truth that the United States had sent missiles and weapons to abet the Afghan rebels and to kill Soviet soldiers, thereby justifying this event as being in our own defense to avoid being killed by enemy munitions. "But if a lie seems preferable," Brezhnev continued, "then let us tell the same lie."

When President Carter, in deepening dismay, indicated that he did not understand, Brezhnev offered him a plan that would somewhat save face and, at least for the immediate situation, provide a less embarrassing way out of this predicament for President Carter. He explained, "Tabas is a desert region and has many sandstorms and typhoons, which are known to cause numerous catastrophic effects. Let us say that a typhoon caused the aircraft to collide, resulting in the loss of life. Further," he added, "using my influence with the Iranian Air Force, I can arrange for an Iranian pilot to come and bomb all the downed aircraft, thereby destroying all evidence of your crime and what you now claim to be my crime. The incident will be buried forever." The phone conversation between President Carter and General Secretary of Communist Party Brezhnev lasted until 6:10 a.m. At 7 a.m., President Carter announced to the world that a mission to rescue the American hostages in Iran had failed due to unformed climatic conditions and that a typhoon had downed the aircraft designated to carry out this attempted rescue. He emphasized that all fifty-three American hostages remain safe and healthy and in Iranian captivity and that he, the president, assumed full responsibility for the failed mission.

President Carter did not win election for a second term, and the reason for this failed bid very likely stemmed from this hostage situation and the surrounding events that have just been described in an apodictic restatement of a situation not usually so described. In addition, Azadeh emphasized that President Carter, through his actions, allowed circumstances to develop that, in essence, gave impetus to Islamic extremism as al Qaeda in Afghanistan, Hezbollah in Lebanon, and Hamas in Palestine (and certain related radical groups in India, the Philippines, Sudan, Egypt, and Sri Lanka). Even Khomeini regarded the sequence of events that evolved from this hostage debacle as a miracle of Allah that eventuated in his being able to spend income from the sale of Iranian oil in support of Muslim extremism.

Six minutes after assuming his presidency, Ronald Reagan announced the good news that after 444 days of captivity, the fifty-three American hostages in Tehran had been released from their bondage and were free! This particular political game of hostage-holding by Iran had ended, but the subjugation of the Iranian people initiated by former president Jimmy Carter in the name of human rights has not yet concluded, and their crisis with an imposed government of inept religious demagogues continues even to this day. (At that time, Iranians were inclined to believe that there would be changes in their Islamic dictatorship through altered global strategies. But this did not happen because, then as now, the influences on Democrats and Republicans were similar as I previously explained; and a Democratic presidential victory in 2008 will probably not change policies in the Middle East very much either.)

In short, politics do not distinguish enemies and friends. For 444 days, the USA allowed their diplomats in Tehran to be taken hostage and then freed them, having worn out any advantage, through deception, any goal that such "captivity" might possibly achieve. The pawns in this political action were the individuals whose lives were held in suspension over this span of time; and ironically, because of the deceit involved, none of the hostages have the right to sue the Iranian puppet regime who were compliant in this hoax of their retention.

In the eight years of war between Iran and Iraq when Western powers had achieved their intentions, President Reagan stated, "I don't understand what this war is about." And Khomeini accepted a cease-fire (1988), and the conflict was ended.

In conclusion, the foreign political strategy of the West, molded as it was by the influence of the lobbyists that I have already mentioned, resulted in the financial and social ruin of Middle Eastern countries—in particular, Iran and Iraq. The politicians of these Western powers knew full well that the destructive results of such machinations would be entirely unacceptable to the average citizens of their countries if they were properly comprehended, so they were the subjects of a hypocrisy and deceit that effectively blinded them to what was really occurring. It was at this point in my discussion with the couple who had been eulogizing Jimmy Carter that they, having listened in apparent dismay, sighed despairingly and hopelessly and said, "Politics is really a conundrum, filled with startling ironies that have far-reaching effects that surpass our wildest imaginings and retrospectively provoke many of our deepest regrets."* To which I can only add what I have previously stated—namely, that Western power politics has no regard for humanitarian rights and needs of those of other nations but operates upon the principle that might is right and upon the Thrasymachian concept of tending to one's own needs and benefits.* If the reader wishes to delve further into and to better understand the complexities and imbroglios of what we have simplistically termed "politics" (oftentimes, the functions of national intelligence agencies is really the warp and woof of our governmental actions), I invite them to read a recently published book entitled *Family Jury*. It is a publication incorporating a compilation of the activities of governmental intelligence agencies between 1950 and 1970, written at the order of James Chelsing, chief of the U.S. CIA in the 1970s, and summarizing various actions of such official groups carrying out what are really unlawful espionage functions that affected citizens of the United States, Russia, and China during that time. In it, there are documentations of hundreds of such activities. Commenting about this publication, current U.S. CIA director Michael V. Hayden indicated that the content reveals shameful violations of civil law, but that they detail infractions of the law that are factually recorded and that are indeed an apodictic commentary upon the history of this intelligence agency.

Really, this Western attitude may also be called racial fascism and is also a type of racial extremism. Racial fascists are concerned only with the needs of their own race, and racial extremists only recognize validity in their own beliefs and are ready to eradicate any who hold beliefs other than their own. Neither approach will solve the problems of today's society nor provide a reasonable solution to the needs of humankind. As previously pointed out, colonization, manipulation, or martial force cannot be the approach to global relations.

Religions that have tribal roots, such as Hebrew and Islamic faiths, have intricate disciplinary rules and regulations designed to control and organize every detail of daily living. But these tribal religions fail to solve the problems of human beings because within their texts, there are discriminatory phrases distinguishing between men and women, between believers and nonbelievers; and there are allowances for slavery and war. Although these tribal religions try to promote justice, in fact, equity derives only from obeying their own prescriptions and proscriptions. And from their very inception, cheese tribal religions have been in conflict with their neighbors (especially true of Islam), so solution of differences is impossible. Even today, the differences between Israel and Palestine seem to render peaceful coexistence impossible.

Again, there are also religions that are basically philosophical (although some adherents believe that, in fact, they are really tribal in origin). The Chinese philosophers believe that those who follow tribal laws with their long lists of good and bad are basically false. For these oriental thinkers, the highest principles of life are simplicity, cleanliness, sincerity, honesty, and truthfulness. Above all, for them, one must be true to oneself as well to others and must demonstrate compassion and kindness in one's relationships. They agree with Zoroastrians that an individual must believe in goodness: "hear no evil, speak no evil, do no evil." And they also agree with these ancient worshipers of fire that one must return good for good and, most certainly, good for bad (to return bad for bad causes chaos, a very dire circumstance). The venerable Chinese philosophers also agree with Buddhists and Jain that one must always demonstrate love and compassion, provide shelter to all, and, most importantly, avoid doing harm to others—especially to animals. As Confucius summed it up, "Do not do to others what you do not want others to do to you."

After considering and reconsidering all the various religious beliefs in today's world, with its progress and technological accomplishments, we once more ask the question, Is there any religious culture that can effectively confront the problems of hunger; the need for clean water; the consequences of unemployment, war and turmoil, AIDS, and other afflictions— all of which we comprehensively termed "human suffering"? It is my firm belief that there is not any situation, however dire and complex, that does not have a solution or several possible pathways for provision of remedy. Having persisted to this point in the reading and study of my preceding discussion, I believe that the reader may agree with me that each individual culture, its philosophy and its religious beliefs, contains both positive and negative concepts even though one's personal preferences tend to downplay the negative aspects.

Certainly, in this twenty-first century, it would be wrong to allow old political policies of enslavement and colonization to persist in our approach to global relationships. That Platonic and Thrasymachian attitude toward others can no longer be employed as it was in the past by kings and other authorities in their effort to rule and control and, "in the name of God," to economically gain supervision over the destiny of poorer and less sophisticated peoples.

Confucius left no written text containing his philosophical understanding, so his followers seem to have had two different opinions concerning human nature. One group appears to believe that human nature is basically selfish, and we human beings seek satisfaction only for ourselves. To change human nature to become compassionate and caring requires special education and appropriate learning. The other Confucian followers believe exactly the opposite: Human nature is basically kind and caring and that individuals left to their own will demonstrate love and concern for their fellow man. Those who behave in a selfish manner are, it follows, doing so quite against their natural proclivities. They also, with a bit of special direction and instruction, will reverse their unnatural selfishness and conform to their better nature and become loving and concerned for the welfare of their fellow man. Our conclusion is that human nature—whether good or bad, at least according to Confucianists—may be sweetened with a little instructive education, gentle and appropriate persuasion, rather than enforced discipline. Spiritual health similarly may be encouraged by didactic means rather than by force.

Conclusion and Solution Letter to Diplomats
Iranians are not Enemies of East, West, or Israel

This correspondence is a letter of petition in behalf of a society which I desire to create, and to be known as the "International Intellectual Society for Freedom (IISF). I direct this communication to the governing bodies and leading individuals of the so-called "super powers" of the world, both East and West. For it is my wish that these governmental entities might alter their attitude toward the people of Iran. I seek to have them end the injustice that has characterized their strategic treatment of my native land of Iran over the past Century, and I ask them to assist Iranian intellectuals in the overthrow of the current Islamic dictatorship The "injustice" that I decry has been rooted in greed for oil, and is treated extensively in my two books, "Letter to Intellectuals" and "Man and God". My further plea is that a truly democratic republic may be established to replace the theocracy that was installed by the West and Russia in 1979. Such an alteration will allow security for Iranians and for the super powers.

I must also assure the people of Israel that the Iranian people have no reason for enmity or conflict with their nation. There are no anti-Semitic feelings rooted in the descendants of the Persian nation. Geographically, we share no border with the nation of Israel, and we have always traditionally had the best economic and political relationships with its people. I reiterate that our Persian inheritance is that of truth, love, and friendship with all of humanity on this planet. The current Islamic regime in no way represents the true Iranian population. We love the people of Israel, and they, in turn, from the days of King Cyrus, have always treated Jewish people with respect and the deepest of admiration. Prior to this imposed regime, our relations were of the closest and most harmonious nature. When democracy is once restored to Iran, there will always be an open door for cooperation and full reconcilliation!

Let us recall also that there is a large intelligentsia in Iran, and along with those who retain their democratic spirit, there is no enmity for the West or East, and full cooperation will take place once the opportunity is provided. And if calamity should plague either Iran or countries of eastern or western mould, thorough communication and corporate endeavor would take place until the adverse conditions were successfully addressed, because the populace on both sides would understand the vital interests of the other and would strive to do that which is honorable and respectful of the rights and needs of the other. Humanitarian concerns would prevail, and equality and brotherhood would shine forth. Mutual concern would engender peace, friendship and love. Indeed, Iranian intellectuals would step forth and demonstrate their feelings of comradeship for all peoples on this planet!

The nation of Iran derives from a bright civilization and has a history of cultural superiority, but is presently a deprived hegemony cut off from freedom and progress, largely because of the greed for oil that has been a blot on its existence. And, due to Iran's strategic position, political strategies of both East and West have been responsible for the exploitation of its rich possession. Our proposed International Intellectual Society for Freedom pleads for an end to these pre-emptory strategies! Indeed, they reflect a big sin*, which must be eradicated. For as long as there is injustice and inequity, terrorism will persist. And military might of whatever degree will not be able to defeat terrorism, but will only create more hatred and misunderstanding!

For a real victory and the end of terrorism, a new means must be found that is fair and acceptable by the majority of people in this world, including, most especially, the inhabitants of the West and the people of the Middle East. We must put aside jealousy, selfishness, malevolence, and prejudice. There must be

---

* Sin= A detriment, something working against the common good; a handicap.

established a democratic rule in Iran! Translated from Persian is the following saying, which captures the sense of my plea:

"It is very nice to be friends with intellectual (knowledgable) people; But, if you have an educated enemy, that is better than an ignorant friend.
The educated enemy will elevate you, but the ignorant friend will kick you and bring you down!"

Above all, we require the full support of the U.S. and its Western allies,plus Russia for we of the IISF feel that this coterie is responsible for bringing the current ruling Islamic regime of Iran to its position of power....an outcome in 1979 of the conspiracy and contrived propaganda of the bloc in the name of "human rights". Certainly, the majority of educated Iranians are unable to effect a change of regime on their own. We believe that the United States and its supporters are able, through the same tactic of political, not military, intrigue to effect the overthrow of this present Islamic theocracy.

Many leaders of Europe and the United States have described Iran as a threat and problem for the world. The logic of these proclaimants is sophist in nature, and with it we could gainsay the intentions of any nation. Because the logic is false, and lumps the Islamic leaders with the true natives of Iran, the conclusion is incorrect. "History has demonstrated that during the past two hundred years Iran has never committed any aggression against any country, large or small. During the two world wars, Iran was NEUTRAL. Nonetheless, in both these global conflicts, the south of Iran was occupied by the United Kingdom, and the north of Iran was occupied by Russia. It seems ironic that those major powers who had traditionally been invaders, occupiers, and colonizers throughout the world continue now to use sophist logic to blind the people of their nations and of the rest of the planet to their clandestine policies in order to justify their continued aggressive strategies." It is not Iran that is the threat, but rather the imposed Islamic leadership of my nation. Indeed, the Muslim hierarchy is a threat, not only to the rest of the world, but also to my very own fellow Iranians! For by these theocratical thugs so many of my brothers and sisters have been stoned, beheaded and flagellated. (Most recently, for example, between January 1st and 8th, 2008, five Iranians in the Southeast Province of Sistan, were declared seditious by the ruling regime and had their right hand and left foot amputated as proper punishment according to Islamic law for their disloyalty! Only one small example of the inequities that exist because of this imposed government.)

The plan proposed by the IISF for overthrow of this dictatorship is shared by many of our membership, and is not just the idea of a single individual. We do not call for a coup d'etat or bloody rebellion, such as was engineered in order to bring the Shah to power (and to bring him down in 1979 and replace him with Khomeini). This singular new plan will be of far greater permanancy, it is hoped. It will be based upon the establishment of a democratic constitution and, thereby, of a constitutional democracy. The imposition of this document will allow Iran to be transformed into a national, governmental entity similar to many of those in Europe, and would allow the Iranian nation to become a trusted political power among the democracies of the world! And, just as a change of the President in Germany, France, or the United States does not alter its basic relationship to the community of nations, so also a change of leadership in Iran would not change its position vis-a-vis the international scene.

The basic tenet of the new constitution would be that no one individual would dictate internal policy. The legislature of this newly created constititutional democracy would be composed of highly educated persons. The ultimate interests of the people of Iran would be the major objective of this document; while foreign interests would also be respected, the emphasis would be upon justice and equality for the Iranian people....an element neglected in the past.

By the formation of this new constitution, freedom for the native population of Iran would be guaranteed, thereby benefitting the interests of all: individuals, religious entities, economic groupings, military echelons, and educational enterprises. By encouraging the writing and establishment of such a document, respect for the United States and the Western and Eastern powers would be restored.

Although I will go into greater details regarding the structure of this proposed new constitution in a second letter which will follow herein, I do want to indicate that part of this document would direct the re-privatization of oil production and distribution, as well as that of the management of all mined resources. Such handling of natural materials would remove control of these resources from the political sphere, and ensure that the technological and engineering expertise of private companies both domestic and foreign, would be the modus operandi in the conduct of these industries. The payment of taxes by these private enterprises would provide the government with compensation and a fair financial interest in their successful operation.

To accomplish the framing of such a constitutional democracy. We will call up on all Iranian intellectuals and philanthropic tendencies of the people of the World, and as well, the idealism of all "first world" citizens. We will also need the spiritual support of all peoples. The economic and philosophical support of the world will enable the initiation of the framing of this constitutional format. Informational technology of the mass media will also have to be called into support, in order that all people in every nook and cranny of our planet will understand the objectives of our endeavor. Public pronouncements by educated Iranians that the end of tyranny "in the name God" is finished and no longer tolerated by the people of "again proud" Iran! The Islamic dictatorship will have been dissolved into freedom!

Ahmad Nosrati, Founder
(Proposed) IISF

To: Governments who are a member of United Nations, specially U.S.A., U.K., France, Russia, China

Purpose of the International Intellectual Society for Freedom:
(Establishing an Iranian constitutional democratic government.

After nearly more than thirty years of exprience with current slamic theocracy in Iran, the total effect upon the nation has been a negative one.   There currently is a high rate of unemployment, drug addiction is at an all-time high, and prostitution exists at an unwarranted level. Many young people feel that their highly motivated aspirations are for nought, and fully eighty percent of youth would prefer to leave the country, were they allowed to do so. The Constitution of the nation is out-dated, for it allows the stoning and beating of individuals, amputation of limbs for crimes of indiscretion, and persecution and killing for opposition to the state...all of these anachronous punishments without due process of court hearings or legal jurisprudence. And when these desecrations of the freedom of individuals are executed, no one stands responsible for the destruction of life and limb that has occurred. Inequalities of gender exist without any protection against discrimination. In short, the Constitution is a Seventh Century document holding sway in the Twenty-first Century, and, as such, is entirely unacceptable.

The International Intellectual Society for Freedom (IISF) wants to establish an Iranian government in exile using as its base the United Nations Charter for Democracy, and establishing its existence with a re-written Constitution that would abolish each point of injustice and inequality that is enumerated in the preceding paragraph that outlines our objections to the anachronous nature of the existing Iranian Constitution. To accomplish this necessary task, the IISF would require at least three to six months in order to contact and meet with all decent Iranians throughout the world (both inside and outside Iran) who stand in opposition to the horrendous injustices that characterize the rule and Constitution of the currently imposed regime in our native land. The composition of a newly devised document guaranteeing freedom and justice for all individuals and religious entities would be the result of the cooperative endeavor that would result.

It is not logical that a nation of freedom-loving individuals be governed under a Constitution that is out-model and based upon principles of the Dark Ages. In the Twenty-first Century both the governing parties and the governed peoples utilize modern means of transportation, such as automobiles, airplanes, and stream-lined sailing vessels, rather than camels and donkeys, balloons, and rowboats. Similarly, law based upon stone age and barbaric principles can no longer be considered acceptable. With modern means of electronic communication it is not plausible that human beings undergo such debasing treatment without recourse to legal appeal and international review.

In the Constitution of the IISF-supported government in several major principles would be emphasized:

1- Majority rule will prevail, but the minority will be respected and never subject to retaliation-of any sort. The idea of getting rid of those in opposition will not be permitted, and there will be no tyrannical treatment of those who have expressed views contrary to the majority. Opposing ideas will be noted and held in alternative reserve, should, by trial and error, the majority opinion prove to have been in error. Resort to change, rather than coup d'etat, will be the modus vivendi.

Propose for the IISF

2- The new democratic Constitution of Iran will respect the rights of all people, even those of the deposed current regime. They and their families will be treated with the same equitable attitudes and access to freedom as those who they formerly governed. They and their families will be safe from discrimination and injustice. Revenge for past misdeeds will not be permitted, and punishment by association will not be allowed. All religious preferences will be respected, and recrimination for previous attachments will be proscribed. The new democratic government will be based on forgiveness and reconciliation. In turn, the current regime of Iran is asked   peacefully to accept the will of the majority of Iranians in instituting this new Constitution. The IISF extends the "olive branch", and for the sake of all humankind, requests the acquiescence of this democratically replaced oligarchy. We insure your immunity to retribution, and guarantee your freedom to enjoy equality in all regards.

3- The new democratic Constitution of Iran will emphasize service to mankind and will maintain human rights as defined by the Charter of the United Nations.

4- The new democratic Constitution of Iran will honor all thirty Articles approved in the United Nations Charter of December 10, 1948. (As Eleanor Roosevelt, the President of the Human Rights Commission, stated, "These are Articles everyone should live by.") Such principles, IISF avers, are "musts" that Iranians should adhere to, if they are to earn happiness and freedom, and are to make progress.

Thus has been outlined the plan of IISF for the peaceful "revolution" that can overtake the struggling nation of Iran. But this proposal cannot be implemented without financial support.

The IISF requires some time (at least three to six months) successfully to contact and meet with all intellectuals, mostly Iranians, both inside and outside of Iran. All who agree that "change" must come to our native land in order for international harmony to prevail must unite peacefully, prayerfully, and politically to draw up and compose our new Constitution. Funds for travel, residency, meals, and equipment to implement such a grand "gathering" are essential and required. for such an important composition to be formulated. Rallying mass media then to communicate this revolutionary concept to all in our nation will then be required, and probably at considerable expense. Every individual and willing organization and country who would lend monetary support for this significant peacemaking effort could look forward, provided its success, to compensation through the commodity of oil, which lies at the base of all of our problems and dilemmas, for a liberated people would gladly share a reasonable portion of its revenue from 4-5 million barrels of oil produced daily from Iran....an amount that might be increased by more than 9 million barrels daily with the application of modern technology..... in order to refund and defray expenses generously contributed in order to accomplish this grandiose scheme.

Please listen to and consider this thoughtful proposal. Possibly the fate of our planet is dependant upon its outcome. Global warming is one kind of threat, but Global negligence is another. If we cannot effect a peaceful solution to today's political conundrum.......radical terrorism versus democratic ingenuity....... the survival of the world hangs in the balance. Let us attempt a solution or be willing to succumb passively to horrendous implosion of humankind.

Sincerely,

Ahmad Nosrati
Founder of IISF

Ahmad Nosrati

Foundational resolution and Statement of Purpose
INTERNATIONAL INTELLECTUAL SOCIETY FOR
FREEDOM

WHEREAS, THE FOLLOWING HISTORICAL
BACKGROUND HAVING BEEN CONSIDERED, namely:
During the time of the Cold War involving the Western Nations
and the Union of Soviet Socialist Republics, political strategists
decided to support extremists groups to limit the influence of
Communism in the Middle East, and especially to prevent the
Soviets from reaching warm water ports of the Persian Gulf and
its oil-rich commerce. In the process, the West trained and fully
armed fanatical Muslim groups.

In the war in Afghanistan, Western intelligence chose to work
with a Saudi multimillionaire and Vahabi Moslem fanatic named
Osamah, with a resistance force named the "Almojahedeen &
TALIBAN Muslim Sunnis" In Iran, the West opted to support
a fanatic of the Islamic Fadaei Party named Khomeini, who knew
very little about economics, politics, or modern diplomacy, and
who was imposed and supplanted by the imperial governmental
regime in order to fulfill Western military and economic strategy
for the Middle East. In short, even though the West is not fond
of Islam, they preferred Islamic instead of Communistic ideology
in the Middle East. They enjoyed temporary success by defeating
Russia in Afghanistan and removing a "thorn in their side" of
the authority effected by Iran. This however resulted in brining
radical extremists to positions of power in both countries, in
the eventual tragedy of 911, and in a trillion plus dollar struggle
causing much loss of precious life and limb in Iraq, as well as in
Afghanistan.

WHEREAS, Western politicians were aware that by establishing Islamic regimes in Afghanistan and Iran they might bring about significant torture, destruction, killing and the curtailment of freedom; Supporting the radicals in the "name of freedom" eventuated in the destruction of the principled ideals of these two nations. Terrorists rose to power in Afghanistan and Iran, a development not possible without the empowerment from the West, WHEREIN THEREFORE, establishment of an International Intellectual Society for Freedom is thus proposed, a group of concerned individuals who believe that compassion and genuine care....even for one's enemies....can be far more effective than pure military might. Some of the Western powers have spent more than a trillion dollars for munitions in the present Iraq war in the cause of freedom. How much have these political powers actually spent for humanitarian concern? Very little, indeed. The International Intellectual Society for Freedom (IISF) must fill this gap by:

1. Promoting true freedom all over the world, especially in the Middle East, thus halting the tyranny and absolutism of dictatorial regimes and of terrorists.

2. Educating people with truthful information that may be supplied by bringing books, documentaries, movies, and other modes of media to the people. Two of such books A Letter to Intellectuals, which discusses the manipulation of Iran by the West and Russia; and Man & God, which discusses truth and reality about religion and political strategy of the West in the Middle East, will commence this effort of truth telling and healing.

3. Assisting people of Iran who are working for freedom in their homeland..

4. Meeting and promoting dialogue with officials in the West and in the Middle East identifying problems and possible solutions.

5. IISF does not work against or oppose any nation or individual, rather the emphasis is concern for all, regardless of race, religious belief, or color. IISF desires open communication among all peoples, reconciliation of enemies, and peace for all. Any support solicited spiritually as well as financially, will be directed to the above goals.

As we have previously suggested, those of the Christian faith approach the solution of human problems with a basic attitude of love and compassion. Christian belief allows for personal freedom for all, with no bias or discrimination. Everyone has equality in the eyes of a loving God, who gave his only begotten son to die in atonement for each individual's sinful nature, if only that individual will profess faith in that son and God's plan of salvation through him. The history of Christianity and its development through ages of challenge and change will now be provided by my friend and colleague Dr. Quentin F. Knauer, who is a physician by vocation and lay pastor in the Christian faith by avocation. He and his wife, Mary, are elders in a Presbyterian church and have had special training for the lay ministry through their presbytery.

Chapter Eight

A Brief Consideration of Christianity

I believe in God the Father, Almighty, Maker of heaven and earth:

And in Jesus Christ, his only begotten Son, our Lord:

Who was conceived by the Holy Ghost, born of the Virgin Mary:

Suffered under Pontius Pilate; was crucified, dead and buried:

He descended into hell:

The third day he rose again from the dead:

He ascended into heaven, and sits on the right hand of God the Father Almighty: From thence he shall come to judge the quick and the dead:

I believe in the Holy Ghost:

I believe in the holy catholic church: the communion of saints:

The forgiveness of sins:

The resurrection of the body:

And the life everlasting. Amen.

The Apostles' Creed, printed above in one form, is the basis of belief for Christians everywhere. In short, we believe in a trinity of divine individuals headed by God, the Father who, while being of no particular form or substance, is reflected in all creation and glorified by all creation. The Son of God, Jesus, is our Savior and has transformed eternity into a glorious life everlasting for those who put their faith in him. And inspiring and making our lives on this earth tolerable is the Holy Spirit, also created by God, our comforter and motivator, vitally filling in where Jesus left off to become our intercessor at God's right hand. The creed also provides an excellent biography of Jesus.

The Christian Church had its inception with the statement of Jesus in Matthew 16:18, "And I also say to you that you are Peter, and on this rock I will build My church, and the gates of Hades shall not prevail against it."

This pronouncement followed upon the response of Peter to Jesus's question, "But who do you say that I am?"

And Simon Peter answered and said, "You are the Christ, the Son of the living God." And indeed, it was Peter who established and built the disciples of Christ into a body that became the earliest Christian Church, centered in Jerusalem. Had it not been for the actions and temerity of Peter—strengthened by the Holy Spirit, recorded primarily in the biblical book of Acts, and following upon his earlier denial of association with Jesus (Matthew 26:69–75)—the fostering and organization of the disciples might not have occurred. It is to this complex fisherman and the presence and intervention of the Holy Spirit that we owe our existence as Christians today.

The growth of Christianity beyond the boundaries of its birthplace can be attributed to the work and writings of the most learned and devout Jewish scholar and contemporary of Peter, the apostle Paul. His devotion to the sharing of the "good news" of the life, death, and resurrection of Jesus Christ with the Gentile population around the Mediterranean Sea is also documented in the book of Acts. His interpretation, application, and expansion of Christian theology is preserved in the dozen or more epistles that he wrote during his heroic ministry and that, as a "man of letters," became his contribution to the developing New Testament, eventually to be canonized along with the writings of several of the other disciples and with the Old Testament of the Hebrew tradition as the Christian Bible.

The impacts of the Pentecostal event described in the second chapter and of the conversion experience of Saul (Paul) recounted in the ninth chapter of the biblical book of Acts supplied a driving force beyond human understanding for the perpetuation of the early Christian Church and emphasized the significance of the miraculous and revelational fomentation provided by the Holy Ghost ("presence" of God) in the inception of this institution. The pervasiveness of love in the theology of Christ is immortalized in the thirteenth chapter of the first letter of Paul to the Corinthians.

The description of the first martyrdom of an individual (Stephen) for the sake of the Christian faith is also recounted in the fourth chapter of the biblical book of Acts. It might be presumptuous to say that the survival of the early Christian Church was carried upon the shoulders of martyrs (those who died witnessing their faith in Christ); but as an outcast sect, extremely unpopular with Roman and other overlords, the profession of belief in Jesus Christ carried with it many dangers to one's sanctity and well-being. The enthusiastic "clinging" to belief in the teachings and promises of one who died ingloriously on a cross was, at the least, a grave challenge to the courage of a person; and the willingness to suffer intense pain for such belief was most certainly evidence of possession by a divine presence that provided far more than mere human resolve and bravado. In this time and country of far more easily maintained Christian belief, many of us shudder when we reflect upon the torture and inconceivable pain that Christians have borne in the past, certainly a further salute to the "power of the wonder-working blood" of Jesus Christ. Reference to Foxe's book of Christian martyrs is most instructive in reminding us of how many and how terribly many did suffer to preserve the faith of our fathers. And currently, when we are awed by those willing to die for a faith and to take the innocent lives of countless others, how much more awesome must it have been to observe faithful dying because of conviction that their belief would actually spare others and promote a fellowship of love and compassion that would eventually prevail and bring in the kingdom of God—an ideal condition of existence promoted by our Lord and Savior, Jesus Christ!

The conversion of the Roman emperor Constantine to Christian faith around AD 313 certainly changed the complexion of global society in favor of Christian love and virtue. The sign of the cross under which the armies of this compelling monarch marched was established early in his career when he defeated his archrival, Maxentius, and had a vision that the cross was to be the signature under which he would triumph and rule. During his reign (AD 324–AD 337), Christianity became a religion of favor, and he himself was baptized into the faith shortly before his death. As the Christian Church grew in power during his rule, disputes arose—among the most serious of which was concerning the question of the Trinity, a disagreement that threatened to split churchmen. Constantine summoned a council of these leaders at Nicaea, and it was out of this convention that agreement and the Nicene Creed were promulgated. Such councils, even as the famous meeting in Jerusalem around AD 50 that heralded peace between Peter and Paul over the matter of whether Gentiles must first be Jews, became a standard method of healing potential rifts in the growing Christian faith; and instruments of reconciliation and/or "creeds" that would determine the way in which Christianity would be directed in ensuing periods of development and expansion.

In order to survive as an instrument of faith and peace in the world, Christianity as a church required the development of an administrative arm to frame and organize its teachings in an authoritative manner. The papacy was therefore established as this instrument of government that traced its origin to the apostle Peter himself, who visited Rome in AD 64. Exactly what formal activity Peter was able to carry out in Rome before his martyrdom at the hands of the Roman emperor Nero is not recorded historically with clarity; but most probably, he established a nidus of followers there who, at great risk, eventually initiated the institution of the papacy that was eventually able to grow and flourish when civil and political restraints were eased during the rule of Constantine. We know that theological writings and teachings of martyred Saint Ignatius, Saint Jerome, Saint Basil, and Saint Augustine were early reflections of a loosely bound collection of clerics contributing to the formation of an ecclesiastical institution to be known as the Roman Catholic Church (see footnote 1); but details as to the life and struggles of these early saints are limited. Nonetheless, they formed a later group paralleling in kind the Hebrew remnant of the Jewish prophets and served to keep alive the burning embers of a faith that would eventually become established as a most significant world religion.

As Christians, we are indebted to the Roman and Byzantine churches for all the labors of the nameless and devoted saints that preserved in writing the indispensible Bible and beliefs that we hold so dear today and much more easily than was imaginable in the past. Countless and nameless individuals survived persecution, hunger, and disease in order to preserve that which we grasp and profess with relatively unchallenged fervor today. Not that our faith is without threat in the present world; but certainly, here in the West, we do not cringe as we call ourselves Christian, whatever our sect or denomination!

As has been pointed out, the dynamic of the Christian Church in society certainly changed after the conversion of Emperor Constantine to the Christian faith, but it is important to remember that change occurred much more slowly back in the fourth century and the hundreds of decades to follow. Without the communication miracles of printing and the even greater electronic advances to which we have grown accustomed in this twenty-first century, transformation proceeded at a much slower pace—in fact, at a snail's pace—so that alteration in the attitudes and behavior of a world leader at that stage in the history of mankind produced changes in circumstances in mostly a local area rather than throughout the realm. In short, the treatment of Christians at the hands of barbarians would require eons of time before there might be any noteworthy modifications toward civility, and the persecution of these adherents of a lonely figure on a cross would continue for many centuries.

Ironically also, as the Christian Church acquired a state-supported position, the institution adopted a political stance not unlike the ruling authorities that threw their support behind it; and the Catholic clergy became much more domineering and "intellectualized," adopting governing positions over and against their lay followers that literally enslaved the latter and that promoted a militancy against rival faiths and ideas that could hardly be likened to the peace and to the kingdom of God that Jesus taught about and strove for during his brief lifetime to describe and teach to his disciples. In short, as the church attained status as an accepted institution, its survival seemed to demand an administrative and authoritarian stance that reflected the politics of the society in which it had achieved recognition; and its role as a suffering servant was sacrificed on the altar of expediency. A hierarchy of controlling officials became established, and the feeding of the flock was often lost sight of amid the need for organization and preservation.

Notwithstanding, there were many devoted intellects who served the institution in very devoted fashion and with sacrificial fervor (and we owe the survival of our Christian faith to these persevering scribes and disciples), but the idyllic picture of the church as shepherd and flock was sometimes blurred and resurfaced as the haves and have-nots.

Although we are alluding in a somewhat superficial and hurried fashion to the church as an imperfect and flawed human instrument, it would be entirely fallacious to leave the impression that the growth of Christianity through the ages was devoid of nobility and humane concern. The Christian doctrine that "God is love" and that one "who loves God loves his brother" pervades all of the evangelistic endeavors of this faith. No other religion has depended more upon the good works of its emissaries than has Christianity. Mission and missionaries are synonymous with Christian faith; and as the gospel message has been carried abroad by individuals such as Saint Augustine of Canterbury, Saints Columba and Columban, Saint Patrick, and Saint Boniface, so also have occurred the simultaneous establishment of schools, hospitals, and other services. And beginning in the thirteenth century, the Roman Catholic Church sent Franciscan and Dominican missionaries to all parts of the world to establish churches and works of compassion that are unrivaled in their effect upon those to whose shores they came.

As the church struggled for its political "breath," somewhat unholy alliances were bound to occur. Two centuries of Crusades marked a struggle for real estate and cost the lives of many innocents in the ranks of Christian soldiers and followers of Islam alike and, in the end, practically settled nothing—except possibly serving as the seedbed for a few of the religious differences and insoluble rivalries that underlie today's conflict for which this text is attempting to find an answer. Possibly, as the effect of this human carnage began to be appreciated from the accounts of surviving Christian soldiers that were shared back at their homes, the zeal for such horrific endeavors diminished; and energies were channeled into more glorious and enduring enshrinements of human capabilities. We turn our interest to the building of cathedrals.

Piles of stones, termed by some as Eben-Ezers, had long been the markers of especially holy ground by the Hebrews, places where God was honored, because it was at such a site that the holiest of holies had deemed to make contact with human beings through a prophet or a patriarch. A home for God had been an enticement for King David; but it remained for his son, King Solomon, to erect such a structure. In many ancient religious expressions, massive structures such as the pyramids of the Egyptians and the ziggurats of the Assyrians and Babylonians were structures where a crossroad between divinity and humanity had expressed itself in the form of a mighty architectural achievement that gave permanency to the memory of that encounter.

So the idea that God might be honored with and within a massive building was a reflection back to ancient times. With the Renaissance of art and scholarship that began to sweep across the civilized world and with scientific developments in engineering and the expansion of imagination through the nascent searching of technicians known as astronomers, gigantic architectural undertakings in the form of Gothic and Romanesque cathedrals attracted the skills of carpenters, masons, and laborers and channeled the energies and creativity of Christian artisans and working people into the dedicated task of saluting and celebrating God, his Son, and biblical heroes in stone, wood, glass, and cement. Such creations were the sweat and toil of many Christian laypeople, whose destinies were much more fortunate to have been utilized in a constructive labor of love than in the destruction and carnage of warfare such as the Crusades.

Examples of these marvelous temples include Notre Dame of Paris; the great cathedrals of Koblenz and of Chartres; the Saint Mark's Basilica in Venice, Italy; and the Cathedral of Seville of Spain. Many of these edifices have been titled "theological encyclopedias" inasmuch as they provided representations of scripture and of teachings of the church in pictorial form for the hoi polloi who were illiterate and unable to appreciate the Bible and the great writings of the ages in written form. Detailed sculptures adorned the facades of these architectural masterpieces, providing intimate details of the exploits of the saints while the multicolored stained glass windows outlined in elaborate fashion the adventures of the patriarchs and prophets, the parables of Jesus, and miraculous events of Old and New Testaments. Such thoughtful, skilled creations informed the masses of illiterate subjects among the peasantry and furnished, as it were, the hidden treasures of the scriptures in a sort of cinematic artistry of the Middle Ages.

Untold lives were lost in the erecting of these architectural masterpieces, but their indestructible buttressed domes and walls provided atonement for sins as the glory of God was captured in mighty monuments of mortar and stone. These havens for prayer and worship humbled the flocks that they shielded and provided industry for the priestly multitudes who maintained them. Environmental catastrophes such as the Black Death of the thirteen hundreds were not to be denied by these mighty walls, but nonetheless, their formidable perimeters and interiors encouraged family survivors with inspiration to go on in the face of the loss of myriads of loved ones whose funerals echoed through the corridors of their hallowed vestries and halls. And they became centers for the special occasions of the church calendar events that became so important in the lives of the flocks of faithful whose social lives and escape from misery cried out for a taste of the kingdom.

Further, they became the focus for the sharing of ideas and of news of the day. It was at the entrance to one of these less formidable bastions of Christianity that the ideas of a German monk were posted for all in Wittenberg to read. *The Ninety-five Theses* of Martin Luther had their first airing in 1517 for the faithful on the door of All Saints' Church of this German village.

Although we are indebted to the Roman Catholic Church for the maintenance and preservation of the Christian faith for over a millennium from the time that it received official sanction of the Roman Empire, as a human institution, it evidenced increasing separation from genuine concern for the welfare of its faithful subjects. It had gradually become, often out of necessity, a powerful political entity that struggled for an autonomy both with and without the assurance of support from the kings and governments upon whose authority it derived its strength. Thus, we see the principle of separation of church and state is necessary for the purity of each.

As previously implied, advances in enlightenment parallel progress in communication; so it is not surprising that at the time of the birth of Martin Luther (1483), the recent developments in Germany due to the Gutenberg printing press were spurring a growth in information sharing and in societal aspirations for freedom in many ways. So it was the education of a youth from Eisleben, Germany, that would eventually lead him from a career in law to study to become an ordained Catholic priest. Early on, he lectured as a professor at the University of Wittenberg; and while lecturing on the epistles of Saint Paul, he became inspired by the Pauline doctrine that the righteous shall live by faith—a grace from God that derives from study of the Bible, which is one key instrument by which God continually strives to save mankind through a belief in Jesus Christ as his Son.

With the mention of the creation of the Gutenberg printing press, we are further reminded of the great impetus that that industrial development had upon the production of printed translations of the Bible, which, in turn, enabled many more Christian lay people to read the "Word of God", or "The Book". Historically, the scholarly translation of the Greek rendition of the Hebrew Scriptures (Septaguint) was the "Vulgate" Catholic version. In the 14th Century, Englishman John Wycliff eventually translated the New Testament Latin Vulgate into English with the noble purpose of informing the laity. Although Wycliff escaped burning at the stake by the Catholic hierarchy, his dead body was eventually exhumed and burned as punishment for his dedicated labor. William Tyndale escaped England and with aid from Martin Luther was able to have his English translation of the Septaguint published at Worms in 1525. After a number of years of clandestine existence, Tyndale was eventually captured by the Catholic Church and burned at the stake in 1536. Miles Coverdale based his English translation of the Bible upon that of Tyndale, the Vulgate, and Martin Luther's German version; he also edited the Cromwell "Great Bible". His living at Cambridge, England, within the relative security of the University, staved off execution as a heretic. Later Bible translations up to the modern times have included the King James Version, the American Version, those of Edgar J. Goodspeed and James Moffatt, as well as the Revised Standard and New Revised Standard Versions. The later editions have all been products of dedicated scholarly intention and, fortunately, not surrounded by the duress of the earlier surreptitiously accomplished scholarship. It is significant to note that, were it not for the courage and sacrificial effort and spiritual persistence of very brave Christian devotees, the course of Christian history would very certainly have been altered and considerably protracted.

When he encountered the "indulgence" of the Catholic authorities as a means for enriching the coffers of the Imperial Church by shortening the sentence of loved ones in purgatory, it was the last straw that broke the camel's back and prompted him to record and have printed his *The Ninety-five Theses,* which were theological queries into discrepancies between that which the Catholic Church proposed and what Luther felt that God intended. Although he did not plan to renounce the Catholic hierarchy and their teachings, this is what the effect of his writings had upon society around him; and in 1521, at the age of thirty-eight, he was excommunicated from the church at the Diet of Worms because of the furor that he had created. This series of events initiated the Reformation and was another element in the explosion of enlightenment, termed the Renaissance, that bridged the temporal hiatus from the Middle Ages to the era of modern times. Other Christian reformers—including Zwingli, Bucer, Hus, and Calvin—followed his lead, but with separate agendas, and gave birth to the major departure of the Christian faith from Catholicism known as Protestantism. Both segments of the Christian Church hold the Bible and Jesus Christ as central to belief but differ widely in matters of governance and interpretation.

Were we to cascade the names of the different derivatives of the Reformation at this time, we would discover that the denominational titles hint at some item in the procedure of the reformed bodies characteristic of a fundamental emphasis in their approach to polity or to worship. Ecumenism allows for a rather easy blending of these distinctions, and there is really little divergence in the basic Christian articles of faith, which is a nicety in any dream for future unity and which may be the only real answer to the dwindling memberships in the Protestant expression of Christianity that is being experienced in the twenty-first century.

But let us not get ahead of our intentions for this special short discussion of Christianity.

There is great value in the study of philosophy for it provides a reasonable framework upon which an individual may approach the matter of living in equilibrium with the complicated world in which we find ourselves. Although philosophical reasoning may not lead a person to a personal relationship with God, the revelation of that creator through the life and teachings of one such as Jesus may be a compelling factor in encouraging an individual to become as much like him as is possible, that is, to become a Christian. Upon such a sequence of events has the church of Christ depended for its growth and development through the years. Advocates of this process known as Christian philosophers have graced the history of mankind down through the ages, and it is to several of these thinkers that we will devote a short consideration in the text to ensue.

Who was he?* The outset of this chapter suggests that his life is outlined in the famous Apostles' Creed that is quoted. His conception and birth (4 BC) were miraculous as stated in the creed. His humble beginnings were not likely to have been interpreted as those of royalty although to the shepherds close to the event and to the Wise Men from afar whose curiosity, along with a unique astronomical phenomenon, led them to the place of his early hours and days of his life; his birth was certainly unusual and special. His parents were devout Hebrews and followed purification and circumcision rituals during the observation of which seers, who were among the most dedicated at the Temple in Jerusalem, recognized his very special persona. He escaped to Egypt with his mother (Mary) and father (Joseph) to avoid the murderous vengeance of then king Herod the Great, returned to a Galilean town near where he was born, and grew up as a carpenter's son. Details of his boyhood and early manhood are lacking although he impressed scribes and Pharisees of the Jerusalem temple when he extended his visit there after his parents, devoutly spending the Passover in Jerusalem, had left to return to Nazareth. Indeed, Mary and Joseph had raised their elder child very well.

As a young man, Jesus dealt with the devil in a forty-day period of temptation. He was baptized by the prophet John the Baptist and was identified by God as "his beloved Son" during this sacred ceremony. From that point on, he spent the rest of his life teaching all whom he met about his Father's kingdom, performing miracles of healing and feeding of his followers and devoting endless hours of training of his disciples, a band of twelve whom he had called from their vocations (largely as fishermen). The basic message that he attempted to convey was that of love and just dealing with each and every human being, which are the fundamentals of life in God's kingdom. Much of his teaching was in parables, using items and situations familiar in the lives of his listeners. He specialized in cheering the sickly and oppressed, in extolling the innocence of children, and in identifying true faith in each person he met.

His lifestyle brought him into conflict with the Jewish religious hierarchy of the day, who refused to recognize in him the qualities of the Messiah for whom the Hebrews had long been yearning. They simply could not see divinity in the simplicity of his life, and a royal militant leader he was not. This hierarchy convinced the Romans that he should be crucified as a criminal and rebel. He survived great torture, only to be killed and then to be brought by God back from the dead in order to send out his devoted followers as evangelists to share the Good News of his life and of life everlasting for all who place their faith in him and in God's plan of salvation for people (as Christians).

Notes

Footnote 1: The Eastern Orthodox Church has been a parallel strength in the survival of Christianity through the ages. Shortly after Roman emperor Constantine sanctioned the Christian faith, he moved his center of imperial operations to Byzantium, renaming it after himself as Constantinople and giving rise to a separate center of Christianity in the East. Geographic and political factors caused the church of the East to remain aloof from the church of the West; and the hierarchical structure was different in that the leader of the church in Constantinople never exercised the same extent of control over its subsidiary centers of worship in cities throughout the Balkans, Greece, and Russia as did the papacy of the Roman Catholic Church in relationship to the churches in the rest of Europe. Eastern Orthodox derivative churches have always maintained their own authority and adopted the language of the Eastern countries in which they became established whereas the churches founded by the Roman Catholic clergy have been subordinate to the ecclesiastical control of Rome and have maintained Latin as the language of worship. And although the church in Rome attempted to exercise authority over that at Constantinople, the affairs of the Eastern wing of Christianity were managed largely at the behest of the hierarchy there. Constantinople and Rome were separate cynosures, and the leader in the East was entitled patriarch whereas pope was adopted in the West.

There were also theological differences that tended to drive the two centers apart. In general, the Eastern Church has persisted in an attitude of considering Jesus as the son of God and as of a different substance than that of God, who remains in the primacy, while the Western version of Christianity has tended to equate God and Christ as of one substance and as both having given origin to the Holy Ghost (a difference in rendering of the Gospel statement in John 15:26). All services in the Eastern Orthodox expression are chanted (usually in the language of the congregation), there is much emphasis upon the use of incense, and religious art is of far greater prominence in the sanctuaries of the East. The Eucharist is accompanied by a celebration reviewing the whole life of Christ, and processional activity is observed more prominently.

The drifting apart before the Middle Ages became a complete schism in AD 1054 when each ecclesiastical authority (East and West) excommunicated the other. Following the Fourth Crusade in the thirteenth century when the Christian armies partially destroyed Constantinople, bitterness between the two bastions of Christianity deepened considerably. Islam captured Constantinople in AD 1453 and held the Orthodox churches in subjection during which time the patriarch of the East was considered the head bishop of the Orthodox churches. As Muslim authority waned in the nineteenth century, a number of churches separated from the church in Constantinople. In 1964, a more liberal patriarch, Athenagoras I, met with the pope in Jerusalem; and the following year, the mutual excommunication was ended. There is currently much more rapprochement between the two divisions of Catholicism; and the Eastern Church, which numbers about two hundred fifty thousand million is a member of the World Council of Churches. It is my understanding that the adherents of Roman Catholicism in the world today number about one billion while there may be about eight hundred million Protestants, making the combined total of those professing Christianity close to two billion in number.

The historic personage in whom Christians profess their religious faith is unique in several ways, one among them being the fact that so much is known of his personal life through its recording in the biblical New Testament. Certainly, the apostles Peter, Paul, James, and John expanded our insight into the exemplary life of this holy individual; and they must be regarded as historically first as well as authoritatively foremost among the Christian philosophers (the authors of the Gospels may more apodictically be considered as historians). The writings of these apostles are miraculously preserved as letters in our scriptures, and of course, they may be the incorporated reasoning of several never-to-be-known thinkers influenced by the love of Christ and inspired by the grace of God. We, nonetheless, attribute their expressions corporately to those whose names have been preserved due to whatever aleatory circumstance fate finally allowed.

It is quite apparent that the writing in this "brief consideration" is not scholarly, and it is quickly admitted that a full understanding of all aspects of Christianity must be derived from reading elsewhere. The author of this book has keen insights and functions as an amazing and humble intellect who has come by his Christian faith in a most challenging fashion, a story that deserves telling in yet another writing. The breadth of his compassion to share the powerful effect of Christianity in his life has prompted him to ask me to provide this brief compendium of our faith because I am his friend and possibly the only one accessible to him at this juncture in his difficult life remotely able to do so. His wisdom is appreciated as correct, so the brief consideration merits continuation.

One of the next great Christian theologians historically is Saint Augustine, a philosophical Christian scholar of the fourth century, whose fortunate conversion to the Christian faith was of major significance in the survival of the Roman Catholic

189

Church. Augustine wrote in behalf of the church. Augustine believed that human beings tended to follow ideals that would promote harmony and that they were inclined to pursue a course of behavior from worse to better, provided that distractions did not intervene. Eventually, he intimated that only a remnant was predestined for salvation, a rescue that was not earned but part of the grace of God. Among his most significant writings were his *Confessions* and his *The City of God.*

He is widely recalled for his emphasis upon the importance of the behavior of the individual in relation to one's fellow humans. Christ is relived in what we do, more than in what we say or preach. Love and compassion are key elements in the living of our lives.

Nearly a millennium later, during a time of intellectual renaissance, there lived an Italian for about fifty years who has been regarded as one of the greatest Christian scholars who ever lived and one of Christianity's most prolific writers. Thomas Aquinas laid down foundational systems of thought that became basic to much reformed Catholic dogma, and his statements have become established as a theology known officially as Thomism. One of his most renowned works is the *Summa Theologica*, an unfinished text that deals with God and creation, human nature, virtue and vice, and the final end of man along with Christ and the sacraments. His untimely death ended a brilliant career of teaching and philosophical reasoning in which theology is emphasized as accessible only through the revelation of God whereas systematic philosophy is available to all men through the senses. Respectful of Aristotelian reasoning, he maintained that existence is supremely achieved (perfected) in the substance of God, who alone creates. Jesus is in the same likeness of God, and immortality of the soul is demonstrable. Love and compassion are ideals of existence.

Christianity has always depended upon the interpretation of individuals seeking to understand the nature and the practicality of a kingdom truly presided over by God, the Father; Jesus, the Son; and Comforter, the Holy Ghost. Approaches to such an understanding have been many and varied; the symbol of the cross has been the stamped across different amendments and modifications of thought and action referable to the time when love came down. The Great Awakening on the expanding continent of America; the social reforms of the eighteenth, nineteenth, and twentieth centuries; and the gradual global racial and feminist emancipation tendencies have all in some way mirrored the tortured image of a solitary figure nailed to two pieces of wood and his empty tomb somewhere in an unidentified bit of real estate in Jerusalem. The word that looms large is "agape."

Whether the existentialism of Kierkegaard, the struggle of Barth and Niemöller against a distorted nationalism of the Gestapo, or the bold excommunication by Patriarch Tikhon of antagonist Communist leaders in Russia, the historical strokes on the canvas of history have imaged in their unique way bravery inspired by the *love* of God for suffering humanity, a compendium of people who experienced the loss of many millions of lives in two twentieth-century conflagrations. And in spite of the fact that much of mankind was forced to take time off to defend freedom and to learn ways to kill "the enemy," there have been some really great thinkers during the past decades who have focused upon theology and the indispensible place of Jesus Christ in revealing the loving nature of God and his relation to humanity.

A few giants among these include the names of Albert Schweitzer, Reinhold Niebuhr, Dietrich Bonhoeffer, William Temple, Rudolph Bultmann, C. S. Lewis, and Paul Tillich—not an exhaustive list, but representative of a broad scholarly clerisy of challenging and provocative Christian theologians. Albert Schweitzer, a musical genius whose organ recitals brought the beauty of Johann Sebastian Bach to many European audiences, forsook the safety and celebrity of a performance career in order to share the healing of medicine in the interior of the African continent as a disciple of Christ. His famous hospital at Lambarene was a laboratory for medical and spiritual support of a hurting populace and transformed a reverence for life into a realistic enactment of healing and hope for many. His theological wisdom was shared in *The Mystery of the Kingdom of God* and *The Quest of the Historical Jesus* while autobiographical writings witnessed globally to the love of God in his own life.

Reinhold Niebuhr emphasized that God was in Christ, reconciling the world to himself. He maintained that we are ambassadors for Christ and that we must immerse ourselves in the society and politics of our day in order to demonstrate discipleship to our fellow beings. The answer to the human enigma lies in the love of God and the forgiveness symbolized by the cross. Major works include *Moral Man and Immoral Society* and *The Nature and Destiny of Man*.. His classes at Union Theological Seminary in New York City were usually filled to capacity.

At one time, Dietrich Bonhoeffer was a student in the classes of Niebuhr and later joined him on the faculty of that famous seminary. He thoroughly espoused the activism of his mentor and colleague, and that was to cost him his life. He identified Adolf Hitler as the devil incarnate, a transformation that allowed him to join in the failed plot to assassinate the dictator, and that led to his death only shortly before the liberation of the Flossenbürg prison where his life was ended—a Christian martyr of the costly grace that his true discipleship would not allow him to escape. Chief among his writings are *The Cost of Discipleship* and a compendium edited by friends after his death entitled *Letters and Papers from Prison*. Prophet that he was, he wrote in the latter work, "Christ suffered as a free man, alone, apart, and in ignominy . . . and since that day many Christians have suffered with him."

William Temple, an archbishop of Canterbury, like several to whom we have alluded, recognized the supreme importance of the individual Christian in society. It is the hard work and sacrifice of those in whom the Spirit of Christ is active that transforms society; progress stems from the fact of compassionate Christians becoming active and assuming responsibility for the political, social, and economic order in which they live.

Although an agnostic for a great part of his earlier academic life, C. S. Lewis became a most effective advocate of caring Christianity as he gradually was confronted with the challenges of life beyond academia. His creative genius allowed him to present the righteousness of Christianity in acceptable fashion, even to skeptics. Noteworthy in this respect were his *The Screwtape Letters* and his *Narnia* tales. He was brilliant as author, preacher, and debater. His outstanding capabilities might have permitted him to amass a great fortune, but his Christian charity compelled him to share a large percentage of his income with those in need. His famous ratiocinative challenge was either that you accept Jesus as the Son of God, or you must regard him as a lunatic. The modest intelligence and appeal of this disciple of Christ ranks him as a modern-day Saint Paul, appealing and reaching out to skeptics, even as his ancient counterpart did to the Gentiles.

With the outlandish suggestion that the recorded Gospel accounts of the New Testament are not historic records of the life of Christ, but rather the theological gleanings of the early Christian Church, Rudolf Bultmann has erupted upon the twentieth-century Christian philosophic scene as one of the most influential religious thinkers of recent vintage. His assumption is that many of the details reported in the synoptic Gospels concerning the biography of Jesus actually reflect the chewing up and spitting out of accounts shared orally and then synthesized into the story of a person that those early Christian Hellenists and Gentiles idealized into a messianic narrative that fit their fondest aspirations for a Lord and Savior. He argues that the outlines of these Gospels are texts for argumentative preaching and teaching and are hardly the substance of an historic epic. His *Jesus and the Word* suggests that the New Testament embodies a prescientific view of the world, a "mythical outlook," and that its message must be cleared of this mythical character (demythologized) before it is communicated to the modern hoi polloi. His approach is to carry out this cleansing not to make religion more acceptable to current religious seekers, but rather to clarify to present-day Christians what their faith really embodies. Although the sense of his extensive polemic has revolutionized modern exegesis and energized the critical analysis of scripture, the question of devout critics is just, Where does one stop and start this demythologization? and What is left that can stand the test of sacredness? How close does one come to stimulating a "God is dead" attitude?

Paul Tillich left his native Germany to escape the deadening effect of Nazism upon intellectual research. His scholastic endeavor was to relate Christian faith to secular thought. In meeting the questions of ordinary people, he drew upon his extensive grounding in the existential teachings of Søren Kierkegaard. The god that the atheist rejects may not be the ultimate, but only a factitious representation that really has no validity. To deny the existence of God may only be denying some commonplace representation of a deity that belongs only to the ordinary, workaday world, and that far misses any real substance of the ultimate. Tillich probed man's anxieties about meaninglessness and death and provided theological solutions to their frustrating consequences. A starlit manger and an empty cross may indeed be the most enduring symbols of a caring god in a world where symbols change from age to age. His *Systematic Theology* confronts all of these issues and much more.

All of the preceding writing summarily confronts a brief consideration of Christianity. Adequately, to consider the faith that was initiated in the Middle East amid the heraldry of angels and the earthiness of shepherds a couple of thousand years ago cannot be so simply undertaken. The joy and suffering that have characterized this unique religious outgrowth have required volumes in the relating and attempted explaining; and such efforts shall, no doubt, go on indefinitely. This "brief consideration" is all too brief.

Jesus gave his Great Commission to his disciples, enjoining them to "Go therefore and make disciples of all the nations, baptizing them in the name of the Father and of the Son and of the Holy Spirit, teaching them to observe all things that I have commanded you; and lo, I am with you always, *even* to the end of the age" (Matthew 28:19–20). This call for evangelization was effectively responded to by the Wesleys in the eighteenth century and more recently, using the power of mass media, by Billy Graham. More people have been converted to Christianity by the Reverend Graham in his city campaigns than was ever conceivable when the enjoinder was delivered. The team approach via radio and television has accounted for the stupendous success of this outstanding preacher, and never before has the message of Christianity been so widely circulated. The Reverend Graham has also been a prolific writer with several books—*Peace with God, The Secret of Happiness, World Aflame,* and *Angels*—to his credit. He has led the way for a religious blitz that is unparalleled in religious history.

Christian evangelization has occurred in many ways and places. A following of significant proportions, the Kingdom of God Movement, has taken place under the leadership of Toyohiko Kagawa in Japan. Educated at Kobe University and at Princeton Theological Seminary, Kagawa survived a very serious illness and devoted much of his ministry to the poor. The Second World War interfered with his ministry; but following the startling events that ended hostilities, recognition of his Christian leadership has been revived, and his stance for the cross as a symbol of love and acceptance of suffering has gained renewed appeal.

The Church of Jesus Christ of Latter-day Saints is an interesting celebration of a ministry of Jesus in the New World, attested to and revealed by one Joseph Smith in the state of New York. His discovery and publishing of the Book of Mormon, its movement of followers westward to Salt Lake City, Utah, and the building of the great Mormon tabernacle there form an intriguing segment of Christian history that attests to the miraculous working out of the love of Christ and its effect in the lives of a unique group of people.

Certainly, there are many intricacies and byways (see footnotes 2 and 3) in a consideration of a major world religion like Christianity, even if only a brief consideration is given to it (such as has been the endeavor of this writing). The emphasis of Jesus Christ and of the Christian religion upon love and compassion for all of God's creation as *the* solution to the global problems of today is an interesting concept and an encouraging attitude worthy of universal promotion. And after all, when you really think about it, that may be exactly what Christ had in mind when he bade farewell to his disciples a couple of thousand years ago back there in Galilee.

Amen!

Footnote 2: Most of the early Reformers of the Protestant movement in Europe in the sixteenth century, certainly Martin Luther, did not wish to be separated from the Roman Catholic Church; but rather, their intention was to revise and improve human relations within the context of the institution. The reaction of the established hierarchy, however, could not let this inner reformation take place for it seemed that that sort of "grassroots" internal revision would threaten the entire status quo. The establishment chose rather to excommunicate the rebel clergy; and that action prompted the local governmental regimes to back their local pastors, further to seal the action-reaction phenomenon into a historic movement that we now term the Reformation, or the division of Christendom into separate Protestant and Roman Catholic entities. And whereas these new Protestant Christian enclaves were eventually established slowly outside the yoke of the Roman Catholic mantle, there soon began to be some reform movements that wanted to extend their freedom from hierarchical domination even further than the original reformers wished, which was a phenomenon that Luther and Calvin and Zwingli had feared might happen. In Europe, the expression of self-rule and personal determinism parlayed itself into groupings that were termed Anabaptists, Hutterites, and Moravians.

These new bastions of theological freedom wanted to interpret scripture more to their own congregational preferences than to dictates of some appointed authorities or councils. And in general, there was the feeling that the sacrament of baptism should be reserved as an adult ceremony, arrived at as a decision arising out of personal growth and selection, rather than a divine miraculous happening that preserved an infant for salvation and protection from the devil. Hence, the general term, "Anabaptist," or "rebaptizer."

Of course, there were many other theological polemics concerning love, family, and communal society that set these more extreme separatist movements apart from the newer Protestant divisions. And when moderate reformers become frightened by extreme reformers, the result is persecution of the latter, who usually are much fewer in number—persecution not only by the less extreme revisionists, but also by the original entity (Roman Catholic Church) from which the moderates were formerly separated. The historical result of this feverish zeal that lost touch with the love of Christ was the destruction of many of these more independent human conclaves and almost the extinction of the Anabaptist movement. A few small pockets did, however, survive. The movement westward eventually brought them to the Americas where they survive as Mennonites, Moravians, and even the more conservative derivatives of the Mennonites, namely, the Amish.

Footnote 3: One of the most exciting incidents of modern Christian faith is the exercise of forgiveness promulgated by South African bishop Tutu as the Old World apartheid social and political attitude was slowly and peacefully engineered out of existence in South Africa earlier in the last century. His monumental nonviolent persistence as chief authority on the

South African council of reconciliation exemplified Christianity in action in a miraculous fashion that exemplifies the meaning of the justice and equity of the Almighty as no other historical event has in recent times. Although true freedom still remains to be achieved in this small African nation, the opportunity to pursue such change has been most deeply dependent upon the Christian insight and perseverance of this Nobel Peace Prize winner (1984). And it is quite certain that the nonviolent struggle in the United States against racism led by Dr. Martin Luther King Jr., a Nobel Peace Prize recipient a generation earlier (1964), provided agenda and influence for this great peacemaker during his Christian journey.

Acknowledgments

The original transcripts of this text were written in Farsi. Dr. Quentin F. Knauer (MD) and Mrs. Mary B. Knauer have my deep appreciation for their aid in translating these writings to English. Their knowledge and linguistic expertise were vital to making this work possible. Without their assistance, these controversial discussions would have been insufficient. Also, I would like to express my special thanks to Dr. Quentin Knauer for his contribution of "A Brief Consideration of Christianity."

Bibliography

Human Freedom and Prestige, translated to Persian by Jamalzadeh (Iranian resident of Geneva, Switzerland). Amir Kabir Publishing Co., Tehran, Iran. 1959.

Shah of Iran, Catherine and Jacques Legrand. Creative Publishing International Inc. 1999.

Azadah, Heshmat Mobasher. Washington DC. 1987

World Guide; Rand McNally. Columbia University Press. Undated.

Encyclopædia Britannica. Encyclopædia Britannica Inc. 1985.

Imam Ali, Hasan Sadr. Amir Kabir Publishing Co., Tehran, Iran. 1963.

Who's Who in the Bible; contributing authors. Publication International Ltd.

Handbook to the History of Christianity. Eerdmans Publishing. Hart, England. 1977.